jennifer

Praise for the Book

Nandita Puri's *Jennifer* tenderly brings alive the life of Jennifer Haynes, a survivor of child-trafficking, as she embarks on a journey to bring together the pieces of her own story amid challenging odds.

Passionate and insightful, this is a story that is both heartwarming and a reminder of the grave shadow of this dehumanizing crime.

—Dr Shashi Tharoor, Member of Parliament
Lok Sabha

Nandita blends powerful truths into a story that shakes our world view.

—Ruskin Bond, Author

jennifer

*one woman,
two continents
and a truth
called
child trafficking*

NANDITA PURI

Published by
Rupa Publications India Pvt. Ltd 2020
7/16, Ansari Road, Daryaganj
New Delhi 110002

Sales centres:
Allahabad Bengaluru Chennai
Hyderabad Jaipur Kathmandu
Kolkata Mumbai

Copyright © Nandita Puri 2020

The views and opinions expressed in this book are the author's own and the facts are as reported by her which have been verified to the extent possible, and the publishers are not in any way liable for the same.
All rights reserved.

No part of this publication may be reproduced, transmitted, or stored in a retrieval system, in any form or by any means, electronic, mechanical, photocopying, recording or otherwise, without the prior permission of the publisher.

ISBN: 978-93-5333-841-1

First impression 2020

10 9 8 7 6 5 4 3 2 1

The moral right of the author has been asserted.

Printed at Parksons Graphics Pvt. Ltd., Mumbai

This book is sold subject to the condition that it shall not, by way of trade or otherwise, be lent, resold, hired out, or otherwise circulated, without the publisher's prior consent, in any form of binding or cover other than that in which it is published.

To the homeless children,
may you all have a home.
And to my parents, my husband and my son
—my anchors and my home.

Prologue

It was sometime in October 2014 when I was introduced to a woman called Jennifer Haynes by my lawyer and activist friend, Pradeep Havnur, who was with Against Child Trafficking (ACT), an organization based in Brussels, Belgium. We dined at a local seafood joint in Mumbai, and Jennifer and her daughter Kassana—who was visiting Mumbai at the time—didn't talk much. A couple of days later, Pradeep handed me a dossier comprising court papers and other documents and some news clippings on Jennifer. 'Read it. It will blow your mind. And then give me your feedback.'

Shortly, I read the contents and was so disturbed that I refused to talk to or meet any friends. And, least of all, Pradeep. I would walk down to the little Cross (enclosed stone structures which dot the suburbs of Mumbai) down the road from my house, spend a few quiet moments and count my blessings. When Pradeep finally called and asked me what I thought of Jennifer's story, I said I could not believe it was true. I told him, 'So much misery cannot happen to one person in one lifetime.'

'Precisely,' said Pradeep and then added, 'And, therefore I want you to write her story. Write a book.'

'Oh no!' I said. 'I don't think I would be able to do that.'

'Think it over,' Pradeep insisted. 'You can if you decide to.'

I have authored several books—short stories, a novel and even a biography. Apart from this, there have been innumerable human interest stories that I have penned spanning nearly two decades as a journalist. But, nothing prepared me for this. I had no idea how to deal with Jennifer's story. It was so hard-hitting, and I found the story extremely disturbing, and hence my apprehension.

Another dear friend, a senior police officer, kept egging me on until I was quite fed up and finally said, 'All right. I am writing it.'

And, so began my journey. With Jennifer. With child trafficking. With inter-country adoption. With child sex abuse. As also with crack cocaine and meth hustling. Being a journalist for the longest time, researching and fact-finding was right up my alley. Also, having written fiction, I enjoyed embellishing hard facts with fiction, a device I used many a time in my newspaper columns to dish out the hard, sometimes bland truth, in an appetizing manner!

On my first meeting with Jennifer at my home, she stared at me blankly and insisted she needed 'to buzz'. I had no idea what she meant, and it made me quite nervous. I discreetly messaged Pradeep and to my relief found out that she simply needed to lighten up with a drink and smoke up a joint (a rolled cigarette with weed and tobacco). I had an old bottle of rum tucked in a kitchen drawer and I poured it with some Coke and handed her a glass.

Taking a sip, she asked, 'Old Monk?' I nodded. Taking another sip, she smirked at me and said, 'Cheap. But it does the trick.'

This meeting was followed by many more sessions over chicken *shawarmas* (her favourite) and rum and Coke at my pad. The next few months were a rollercoaster ride as I got to know Jenny, her nature and her mood swings. Some days she turned up late, on others she never showed up at all. Occasionally she would drop off packets of meth at my place, and I would have to chase her to take them back with her. I also visited her birthplace Ambernath and her current home in Thane, Mumbai.

I visited drug dens with her, although as an undercover, and on these occasions my cop friend accompanied me in plain clothes, fearing for my safety. Little did Jenny know of his real identity and assumed he was my boyfriend. We let her think thus, having a hearty laugh between ourselves. And, so with Jenny, I revisited her early days in Mumbai.

As I got to know Jennifer, her family (Judy and Justin, the latter through his prison code mails) and her friends (Austin, George,

Julietta and others), she became almost family to me. And like most family, I was at the receiving end of her many mood swings. There were days when she was normal, abusive on others, and on some others, downright nasty. She would confuse her folks by telling them one day to cooperate with me, and another day, not to. This went on until we finally accepted that this is how Jennifer is. She would disappear for weeks together and then surface again saying she 'went hustling'. I tried to discourage her from doing this as there were chances that she may never return; also, it would do no good to the book.

Easier said than done.

'What do I do to keep my body and soul together till you complete that friggin' book of yours?' Jenny would retaliate. Temperamental as she was, there were times she would scream at me to throw her story away, and then at other times, she would be vulnerable and scared about her jobless state, her mounting bills and so on. Sometimes, she would even pray that she died and it jolted me with fear for her life.

But despite the odds, we managed to survive each other. Sheepishly, Jennifer would apologize saying, 'Carry on, Naaeeta [that's how she always mispronounces my name]. I know you are trying your best to help me reach home.' And, the most touching friendship note I received last year was from Jenny, 'Happy friendship day, dude.' It made my day.

Yes, I am trying my best. Yes, Jennifer's story and life disturbs and bothers me all the time. Yes, I want Jennifer to be with her family. And like her, many more Jennifers must find their families and find peace. It is when I see Jennifer, I realize how lucky my life has been and perhaps, it is my time to payback to society.

Dealing with Jennifer was an eye-opening experience. With its many moments of highs and lows, good and bad, I have been privy to Jennifer's many mood swings. Her impression of me changed with the changes in her mood. One day, I am 'the kindest person' and then on another, 'totally bogus and fake'. I was 'a damn good writer' on certain days and then on others, 'completely useless'. Her memory varied too, and so it was 'crystal clear' on some days, on others, she couldn't remember 'a damn thing'. Incidents, names and dates would oscillate from meeting to meeting. It was dizzying for me to keep up with her mood, memory and facts!

There were days she left me upset and I would turn to Pradeep and his colleague from ACT or Arun Dohle, (who is himself an inter-country adoptee but unlike Jenny's, his story had a happy ending) or my 'cop boyfriend'. As my 'cop boyfriend' tried to explain, 'You must learn to ignore her jibes. Try and understand that she is a disturbed soul. And sometimes it is not Jennifer but the weed talking.' As for Pradeep, and sometimes Arun, they constantly played arbitrator as they were the only people Jenny never spoke ill of.

In the end, I did finish the book, which was my motivation from the very beginning.

I remember asking Pradeep why he chose me to write Jennifer's story. I got so involved that for the past three-and-a-half years, I have not taken up any writing assignments but this. Pradeep said to me, 'We lost the case in the High Court and Supreme Court. But I know Jennifer will go home to her family one day. And I know your book will help her achieve this.' I don't know whether I am worthy of such faith. All I can do is try my best.

Happily enough, the best compliment came from the subject herself. At a local café over a Frappuccino, I let Jennifer go through the first draft. She made a few pencil corrections and then her dark face lit up after going through a few chapters. She smiled with joy and told me that she liked it. 'It's good, man, it's good. I like it, dude.' I thought she was being polite until Pradeep forwarded Jennifer's text to me the following day. It read: 'Once I read it, I couldn't stop. I was reading it like it was somebody else's story...and if she can make the film, f**k it, it will fly. I don't understand why she is taking so long...'

All Pradeep replied was, 'Patience, Jennifer.'

If Jennifer felt the manuscript was so good that she could not stop reading it, it is because her story is almost like a movie unfolding before your eyes. It was riveting and at times, unbelievable.

In this journey, Pradeep and Arun have constantly helped me with information. When I thanked them, I remember Arun once just blurted, 'Don't say thanks. We need to get the story out.' And that hit me hard.

'All women in all cultures are offered a deal', the late Academy Award winning filmmaker and friend, Mike Nichols once wrote to me, 'And a very few can take it and of these, a very few survive.' To me, Jennifer is one of them.

Mumbai 2019

1.

'I was walking like a penguin with my feet chained and carrying a garbage bag across my back. I was looking like a fuckin' Santa Claus. An Indian version of Santa Claus.'

❦

'This is a call for Jennifer Haynes. Will Jennifer please report to the office?' The announcement was loud and clear, and went ringing through the walls of Calhoun County Jail.

Sitting in the recreation room of the jail was a sharp-featured and dark-skinned young woman in her mid-twenties who looked up sharply. She appeared a lot older than her age. At 5'3", Jennifer was rather short by average American standards, and coupled with her shiny wheatish complexion and voluptuous body, she looked straight out of a Khajuraho frieze.

It was afternoon and Jennifer was playing Scrabble with a fellow inmate after her lunch at the Calhoun County Jail. She looked up at the microphone speaker placed above and wondered why she had been called. She could barely gather her thoughts together when in walked Teresa, the attendant supervising the basement floor of the jail which housed Jennifer in Pod E. Along with Teresa was a rather stern-looking, middle-aged white American officer.

'Ms Haynes, please get everything together,' the officer said. Jennifer was asked to change out of her orange pyjama-shirt jail uniform and into regular clothes.

'I am going home, ain't I?' Jennifer asked.

'Hey Jenny, I dunno. Come on. Pack up,' Teresa slapped her in a friendly manner.

'Whadyya mean? You dunno?' Jennifer asked surprised. 'Where am I going?'

'I ain't telling you nothing coz I don't know nothing. Martha's come to take you to Detroit. So you better get packing right away.'

'But why Detroit?' Jennifer asked, perplexed. She knew that the main branch for Immigration Appeal was in Detroit.

With a few letters from her husband Justin Haynes—who was then serving his term at Newberry Correction Facility in Michigan—put in a huge blue see-through plastic garbage bag, Jennifer walked out of Pod E of Calhoun County Jail. It was the morning of the 29th day of June 2008.

❦

After a two-and-a-half hour journey to Detroit with a dozen other prisoners and a few guards in a van, Jennifer reached the Detroit Holding Cell, which was a holding place for law-breakers and illegal immigrants.

Little did Jennifer know what was in store for her in Detroit.

The next day she was made to sit with a number of illegal immigrants, mainly Mexicans, and Jennifer wondered why. After all, she was an American citizen.

'Where are you from?' she remembers Judge Hackett asking her over the television monitor.

'Battle Creek. Michigan.' Jennifer replied.

'I am asking you, where are you from? Which country?' Judge Hackett repeated rather firmly through the monitor.

'The United States of America,' Jennifer replied with confidence and defiance.

'Please don't waste my time, Ms Haynes. I am asking you for the final time. Which is your country of birth?'

'India,' Jennifer whispered limply. 'But, Your Honour, I am...'

Judge Hackett cut Jennifer mid-sentence and said, 'Alright. Ms Jennifer Edgell Haynes is to be deported to India as her papers are not in order. She continues to be a native and Indian citizen, and a resident of the United States, convicted of aggravated felony. In spite of having lived in the United States of America for more than two decades in various state foster homes and adoptive homes, she has no legal documents supporting her as an American citizen. She, therefore, must be deported to the land of her birth i.e. India at the earliest as she continues to be an Indian citizen and has overstayed her visit in this country without relevant legal documents, thereby making her stay illegal.'

It was 30 June 2008 when Jennifer was served her deportation papers to India, a country where she was born, but a country which disowned her and of which she had no memories of since she left it twenty-one years ago as an eight-year-old girl. A country she had no association with; a country she had no fondness for. Just a name on a map, and one she learnt in her Geography lessons in American schools.

Despite Judge Hackett's pronouncement of her deportation, Jennifer felt that she would not be deported. She could not be. After all, she was as American as the plump, short-cropped haired, white American judge. She grew up in the US of A, married an American citizen and had two lovely children from him, who were as American as could be. How could they deport her then?

Jennifer was numb. Her deportation orders did not register in her mind.

For the next two days she was holed up in Detroit, not allowed to call her family or her lawyers.

Coincidently, her case had also been argued at the Supreme Court in Washington DC in the middle of June 2008, as she had served one-and-a-half years of her two-and-a-half-year sentence of probation for possession of narcotics. This was a minor offence of personal possession of more than twenty gram of crack cocaine in 2005. In fact, she jumped probation and, since she could not pay up the US$1,000 fine, she was serving her three months for defaulting on the fine. She had voluntarily given herself in. It was during this time that the United States (US) immigration authorities stumbled upon the fact that her papers were not right. In fact, they never were.

Jayjay, an immigration officer was the first to discover that Jennifer Hancox Edgell Haynes was not officially a US citizen. In Calhoun County Jail, Jennifer was a very difficult inmate to deal with. According to her, she abused fellow inmates and even jail officials and so was always in their bad books. Many a time, she was put alone in a cell due to her difficult behaviour. Jayjay's suspicion was aroused when he found out she was going by three different surnames: Hancox, Edgell and Haynes. He decided to find out more and while researching on Jennifer's past, stumbled across the fact that she was an illegal citizen in the US.

Jayjay also tricked her into signing some legal documents and papers assuring her that if she signed the papers it would facilitate her early exit from jail and simplify her case. Being naive in legal matters, Jennifer signed them, little realizing that she had been tricked into signing her deportation papers.

'I had no idea they were deportation papers,' Jennifer says. 'I could have asked for repeal as my case was already coming up for hearing in the Supreme Court. I could have fought my case on humanitarian grounds. But I was just ignorant and by signing those papers I accepted the two aggravated felonies as well as the responsibility for being an illegal citizen due to incomplete documents by my adoptive parents.'

'That mother***er Jayjay did me in,' says Jennifer after all these years.

On 2 July, Jennifer was informed that she would be flying the same day to New York and then onwards to India. Coincidently, it was also the day of her sixth wedding anniversary.

The first thing she did was to call her mother-in-law Judy Cobbs, who was in Chicago. While Jennifer was serving her jail term it was Judy who looked after her children, four-year-old Kadafi and three-year-old Kassana.

'Don't worry, Jen. I will do all I can to help you dear.' Judy said. But, both knew it was too late.

The next thing Jennifer remembers was being put on a flight to New York accompanied by two male security guards with her hands and feet shackled.

'Care to tell me where am I headed to?' Jennifer asked neither of the two guards in particular.

'New York,' replied one.

'Yeah man, I know it's New York. I heard the announcement. I am not deaf', Jennifer said. 'Where in New York? I need to call and tell my mom and my lawyer.'

'Honey,' said one of them, 'You are not going to stay in New York if that's what you're asking. You gonna be deported to India.' He smirked.

'What the f**k? You gotta be kidding man! You're joking.'

'No. Not me. I don't joke.'

'Alright then, let me call my mom. I need to inform her,' Jennifer said, still not quite comprehending what she just heard. 'I need to talk to my babies. I need to make a phone call home.'

'Sorry, Miss. No phone calls. Not allowed. Strict orders.'

'You must be friggin' joking!' Jennifer exploded as the implication of being deported dawned upon her.

'Sorry. No go. Am helpless Miss,' the guard shrugged.

The guards accompanied her to the plane and then left. During the flight to New York, her handcuffs were removed.

On arrival at the JFK International Airport, two other security guards from the Immigration Department took over.

'I'm hungry. Are you gonna feed me?' Jennifer asked as they led her on at the airport. Her mind had stopped thinking after getting the shocking news of her deportation. She arrived like a zombie on autopilot to New York. She needed to keep herself engaged in order to keep her mind numb. Meanwhile her hunger pangs arose.

'I'm hungry. Can you get me something to eat?' Jennifer asked.

'Sorry Miss. We don't have the budget for food,' one of the guards said, suspicious that Jennifer may try and attempt to escape on the pretext of being fed. 'You will be fed on the plane.'

'I don't give a damn. I am so hungry I will collapse. The bloody flight has been delayed by two hours and I will not be able to hold up that long. I am thirsty too...I am gonna tell the world you prigs are denying me my basic rights to food...'

'Alright. Alright, Miss. Let us see what we can do,' one of them tried to calm her down, fearing she might create a scene in the busy JFK terminal. They had been forewarned about her difficult behaviour.

Finally, one of them got her a Bean Burrito from the Taco Bell counter. Her handcuffs were removed and she was allowed to eat. However, her feet remained chained.

As the flight was announced for boarding, Jennifer was awakened from her slumber at the airport couch, where she had dozed off under the supervision of the guards. The news of deportation two days back had come as such a shock to her that she had not believed for once that it would be implemented. She had been living in a state of self-denial.

She woke up to the stares of the people as the guards steadied her up. With her hands and feet chained and the huge garbage bag slumped across her shoulder, Jennifer made for an awkward sight. 'Those bastards wouldn't even help me carry my sack. At least those jailors could have given me a decent bag to carry my stuff instead of a friggin' see-through garbage bag,' Jennifer recounts, fuming after all these years.

'I was walking like a penguin with my feet chained and carrying a garbage bag across my back. I was looking like a fuckin' Santa Claus. An Indian version of Santa Claus.'

※

2.

Human trafficking is an ancient trade. A lucrative trade.

In ancient times, people mainly acquired their slaves or domestic workers from war conquests. In Imperial Greece and Rome, human trafficking was a thriving and profitable industry. Slaves were treated with cruelty and were flogged for every small error in the most inhuman of ways. Most of these slaves were from African and Asian countries and were bonded labourers for life. This sort of bondage was a part of ancient cultures such as in Egypt and India. Even the Hindu caste system practised slavery under the garb of religion.

It was around the fifteenth century that slave trade became global, and slaves were imported from country to country. Thus, inter-country slave trade became a thriving business and the economies of a number of European cities were based on slave trade, and it began to be accepted as an important part of national and commercial interests.

In the eighteenth century, Reformist thinkers such as Voltaire and Rousseau, helped curb and finally eradicate slavery through their writings and advocacy. The worst form of slavery was blatantly practised in the southern states of the US, until it was finally abolished in 1865 with the 13th Amendment to the US Constitution.

The 1948 Declaration of Human Rights banned it completely, and today slavery and human trafficking is forbidden worldwide. In reality, however, it is a different story.

According to the International Labour Organization, more people are enslaved today than have been at any other time in human history. Allegedly, an estimated 5.5 million children are engaged in forced labour worldwide.

In 2006, some people accidentally stumbled upon the ancient Mayan 'Midnight Terror Caves'. It was then proved that even as far back as 1200 years ago, roughly between AD 250 and AD 900, a trade network dealing in child trafficking existed. The ancient Mayans were a ritualistic people and worshipped Mother Earth. To appease the weather Gods, especially the Rain Gods, the Mayans made offerings to Mother Earth, which included crops as well as human sacrifice. Most of the human sacrifices were children because of which child trafficking was a profitable trade.

While human sacrifices constituted the primary cause of child trafficking and slave trade in the past, children were also bought and sold for sexual exploitation and for use as slaves (or, what we today refer to as child labour). These same reasons have seeped into the present age where trafficking of children and adults has reached its peak in terms of statistics. Today, apart from sex abuse and forced labour, children are also victims of organ trade.

3.

Seated in the first row of the first class of the Delta flight from New York to Mumbai, Jennifer was in a daze. Her surroundings looked posh and luxurious. Her passengers, whom she looked at from time to time, looked very stylish and rather snooty. There was nobody seated next to her and the seat remained vacant throughout. Across the aisle from her, there was an elderly couple. The lady was dressed fashionably and had already settled in her seat, leafing through a copy of *Harper's Bazaar*, her reading glasses perched on the tip of her nose.

Her lips were scarlet. Next to her was a balding gentleman, most likely her husband, casually reading a newspaper wearing a heavy gold Rolex. Like the one Justin wore, thought Jennifer, except that Justin's was a fake and this must be the real thing. Both of them stole glances at her.

The air hostess had settled her in and belted her in her seat. Her handcuffs were removed by her guards and the keys were given to the air hostess. Jenny was offered a glass of water, which she refused. She was then offered a glass of orange juice. She hesitated. She saw another flight attendant offering Mr and Mrs Scarlet Lips wine, or perhaps champagne—Jenny could not tell. 'I want a glass of that wine,' Jenny pointed it out to the air hostess.

'Sorry. You cannot have that. That is champagne,' the air hostess replied.

'Why not? I am flying first class like the rest, ain't I?'

'Yes. But, I have strict orders not to serve you alcohol,' the air hostess replied. Sylvie was her name or at least that is what the badge on her blouse said. 'Anything else you need, you ring the bell for me. My name is Sylvie,' she pointed to the bell above. 'Tea, coffee, soft drinks, food, anything, anytime.' Sylvie smiled. She showed Jennifer how to unlock her seat belt once the seat belt sign was off.

'Hey what about taking off the chains from my feet? They hurt.' Jenny asked.

'Sorry. No go on that one. We have instructions not to take them off till we land in Mumbai. You need any help going to the toilet, just ring for me.' Sylvie smiled.

Damn. Jennifer needed a drink badly. She needed to steady her nerves. It was finally dawning upon her that she was being sent to India. Far, far away from her home. Away from her family, away from her friends, and away from her two little babies, Kadafi and Kassana, who were her world.

Those assholes, Jenny thought to herself, did not even give her time to meet her family. She wanted Judy to bring the kids to her so should could give them one tight hug before she was taken to India. But that was not to be. Before she or Judy realized the impact of her being deported, she was bundled off from Battle Creek to Detroit, then from Detroit to New York and finally onwards to Mumbai. All this within a span of 48 hours! She so badly wanted to meet her children.

After the plane was cruising and the seat belt sign was switched off, Sylvie came and unclasped her belt. She asked her if she needed to use the toilet. Jennifer refused. In fact, she never used the lavatory during the entire twelve-hour flight. She was given a magazine to read and offered some soft drinks. Jennifer opted for a Coke. While she munched on some pretzels and leafed through the flight magazine, Jennifer decided to watch a Bollywood film. Jenny had heard about them from her Indian friends in Battle Creek though she never watched one herself. She had heard about Amitabh Bachchan and Shahrukh Khan, the famous Bollywood stars. She decided to watch a film and Sylvie helped her with this. Over dinner, she watched a full-fledged Bollywood film replete with songs, dances and action—the works. 'I can't remember exactly, but I think it starred Akshay Kumar and Rani Mukherji. I may be wrong though. But, it was entertaining and kept me distracted at the time,' Jennifer recollects.

'I had no idea about India or Mumbai. I wanted to find out about it. There was an Indian boy coming out of the toilet who sat behind me. I smiled at him and gestured him to come towards me, which he did. My feet were covered with the airline blanket so he could not see my chains. I told him I was nervous as it would be my first visit to India and asked about the weather here. He said it was raining a lot, and it would be wet and slushy as the monsoons were on. He asked whether I was going for a holiday or visiting friends. I told him I was being deported and removed the blanket to show him the chains. He immediately left. And that was the end of my lessons on Mumbai,' Jennifer laughs.

※

Mumbai, the capital of the state of Maharashtra, lies on India's west coast by the Arabian Sea. It is a cluster of islands and derives its name from the local goddess Mumbadevi. When the Portuguese ceded the group of islands to Charles II of England in 1661 as dowry for Catherine de Braganza, the name was anglicized to Bombay. The name of this city was changed to Mumbai in 1995.

Today, it is India's most densely populated city and the world's fourth. Besides being famous as home to Bollywood and its stars, the city is also the financial capital of India. People from all parts of the country come to make their fortunes here.

※

On a rain-washed day in July, Jennifer Haynes landed in this city of dreams.

She was the last to get off the plane when it landed at the Chhatrapati Shivaji Maharaj International Airport in Mumbai (formerly Bombay). Like the city, the international airport was earlier known as the Santa Cruz Airport, named as part of its Portuguese heritage. It was later renamed to its present tongue-twisting avatar due to local political backlash. The regional politics of Maharashtra had decided to disown its Portuguese and British influence by going back to its Marathi roots.

As the last of the passengers from the business class had left the aircraft, Jennifer was led out by Sylvie who had a yellow envelope containing all the relevant documents for her to enter India. Sylvie handed the papers to a Mumbai police officer, who then made a few calls and told her that Jennifer was to be returned to the US.

On hearing this, Jennifer's eyes lit up with happiness for a brief moment. But, it did not last long as a senior officer came in and said that the papers were in order and he had received instructions to let her go.

'You can go now,' he told her.

'Go where?' she asked, still dazed. Her feet were shackled and people stared at her.

One of the local security guards unlocked the chains from her feet.

'You are free to go wherever you want, Madam. You are free now.' The officer said.

For the first time in 48 hours, Jennifer was free of her shackles. But, she still could not revel in her freedom, trapped as she was in a world she had no idea of.

※

Jennifer Hancox Edgell Haynes was free to go wherever she wished but in reality she had nowhere to go. And that was the irony of her life as she stepped on Indian soil.

She walked around the airport for a bit and then sat down in despair. She had no idea where to go or what to do. After an hour or so, having freshened up at the airport washroom, Jennifer started planning her next move. The only person she could think of to bail her out was her mother-in-law, Judy Cobbs, far away in Chicago. She needed to get in touch with her. But, without a penny in her pocket, there was no way she could call Judy.

Suddenly, she had an idea. She walked up to a police officer who kept looking at her from time to time, and in her best American English explained her plight. He seemed to empathize because he gave her a five hundred rupee note and directed her to a payphone to call home. Jennifer called up Judy and told her to immediately wire two hundred dollars at the Western Union kiosk at the airport. The police officer got her the money and when Jennifer tried to return him his five hundred rupees, he refused at first but later took it. Maybe the kindness of the policeman gave Jennifer hope that she would be able to survive in this country, which was completely alien to her.

She called up Judy again who meanwhile had found out about the Young Men's Christian Association (YMCA) in Colaba from the Internet and gave Jennifer the address. After almost four or five hours at the airport, Jennifer took a prepaid taxi and headed to YMCA on Merryweather Road in Mumbai.

Philip, the manager of YMCA, was at the front desk when Jennifer walked in. Philip was quite used to hippies and tourists with knapsacks on shoestring budgets staying in YMCA. But, he was in for a shock when he saw Jennifer walk in with a garbage bag. When Jennifer could not produce a passport, as she had none, Philip refused to let her stay. Jennifer then showed him her papers given by the US authorities, but Philip remained unmoved. It was almost 3 p.m. and Jennifer was famished. Jennifer then called Judy and made her convince Philip. Judy explained the situation and said she would wire money immediately through Western Union to ensure Jenny's month-long stay at YMCA.

'She needs to figure out her life. Please Philip. Give the child a room,' Judy convinced Philip.

Once Jennifer was shown into her room, she immediately went down to the dining room on the ground floor and had a chicken club sandwich and drank a tall glass of cold coffee. She then went back to her room and showered and changed into the only other outfit she had. She would buy a couple of t-shirts and a pair of trousers later, she thought to herself. She was feeling fresh after the shower. She stepped in the room, and she sat on her bed and before she knew what hit her, she had fallen asleep. Jet lag hit her hard. It was midnight in Chicago.

Jennifer did not know how long she had slept. It was dark outside. She made her way to the switch and put on the light. The room was small and rather dull. The light did not help make it any brighter.

Jennifer suddenly felt a little lonely. She reached for the remote and switched on the television. The sound of it brightened the little room.

The sounds emanating from the television were alien to her. She could not make sense of what was going on. She changed the channel. This one too sounded strange. She changed to another, then another. She kept changing channels and all sounded alien to her. Finally, she stopped at a channel playing some Bollywood song and dance. She stared at it for a while.

And, then reality hit her hard.

'Damn!'

'I am in India. I have been deported.'

And for the first time since she received her deportation orders, Jennifer Haynes bawled her eyes out.

4.

There are more slaves in the world today than ever before in the history of mankind.

Apparently, of all human-trafficking cases, one-third comprises children who are used for sex trade, child labour and various other crimes. Of this, half are females. Since human trafficking is an invisible crime, it is therefore hard to get exact statistics. A large number of children trafficked for sex die each year due to abuse, disease, torture and neglect—some as young as four or five years old. Apparently, more than 30 per cent of all trafficking cases between 2007 and 2010 involve children being sold into the flesh trade. It is believed that a human trafficker earns double the amount for a girl child than a boy.

Today, the percentage of women in human trafficking far outweighs men. Another trend is the trafficking of pregnant women for their newborn babies. These infants are then sold in the black market, and the profit is divided among the traffickers, doctors, lawyers, immigration officials and others, with the mother getting a measly amount.

Another alleged area for trafficking children is for their use in the military, especially in militant outfits in regional conflicts. A glaring example is the Taliban. According to an article in *The Washington Times* in 2009, the Taliban buys children as young as six and seven years old to act as suicide bombers.[1] The price for child suicide bombers is allegedly anything between US$10,000 and US$20,000. More than 30 million children have been exploited through human trafficking,[2] and a majority of them have contracted HIV due to forced sex with multiple partners. More than 71 per cent of trafficked children show suicidal tendencies.[3]

Today, slaves are cheaper than they have ever been in history. The population explosion has created a great supply of labourers, both adults and children, and globalization has created a section of people who are vulnerable and easily enslaved.

Human trafficking is one of the fastest growing criminal enterprises because it holds relatively low risks with high profit potential. Trafficked children top the list as they are more vulnerable, naive and less risky to deal with. Unlike drugs, humans can be sold repeatedly and this attracts criminal organizations to this trade.

International trafficking is impossible without the connivance of top government officials and powerful people. Because it is such a

---

[1] Staff Reporter, 'Exclusive: Taliban buying children for suicide bombers', *The Washington Times*, 2 July 2009. Available at <https://www.washingtontimes.com/news/2009/jul/02/taliban-buying-children-to-serve-as-suicide-bomber/> Accessed on 7 Nov 2019.
[2] Natalie Cochran, 'A hidden crime: 30 million victims trapped in human trafficking', Lone Star Legal, 30 July 2019. Available at <https://lonestarlegal.blog/2019/07/30/a-hidden-crime-30-million-victims-trapped-in-human-trafficking/> Accessed on 7 Nov 2019.
[3] Cheryl Knight, 'Facts about Human Trafficking'. Available at <http://www.care1.org/617-2/> Accessed on 10 Nov 2019.

lucrative business, there are highly placed and educated people who are involved in child trafficking worldwide. These allegedly include royal members, politicians, bankers, hedge fund owners, professors, scientists and other successful professionals.

Brazil and Thailand are generally considered to have the worst child sex trafficking records.[4] The highest number of orphans is apparently found in Africa due to the AIDS epidemic, while the largest number of child sex workers in India comes from across the border in Nepal.

Human trafficking is one of the greatest human rights challenges of this century, both in the US and elsewhere.

5.

Jennifer woke up the next day still dazed and very confused. Ever since she got her deportation orders in Detroit, she was on autopilot mode for the next 48 hours flying over cities and continents. It was not until she saw the Hindi channels on the television in her room in YMCA did reality hit her.

'I realized I was in a different space.'

During her early days in Mumbai, Jennifer told herself that she had no option but to make the most of her life in this alien city until she could return to the US. She knew it was not her fault that her papers were not right. She knew she would return to the US eventually—India could never be her home forever. Home was where her family was. Home was where her friends were.

Most days Jennifer watched inane television programmes until

---

[4]Policy Analysis and Research Branch of UNODC, 'Global report on trafficking in persons', February 2009. Available at <https://www.unodc.org/documents/Global_Report_on_TIP.pdf> Accessed on 4 Nov 2019.

the wee hours of the morning. Those were the only hours she could talk to Judy, or hear the babbles of Kadafi and Kassana. She slept late and would get up during lunchtime. By afternoon, if it was not raining, Jennifer would scour the by lanes of Colaba and walk along the Colaba Causeway nearby. The weather in Mumbai was warm and sultry despite heavy rains that sometimes continued for days on end.

Originally one of the seven islands constituting Mumbai, Colaba was known as Candil in the sixteenth century when it was under Portuguese rule. When Charles II leased it to the British East India Company in the seventeenth century, they called it Colio. The local inhabitants of the fishing village, the Kohlis, called it Kolabhat from where it derived its present name. As a fishing village, Colaba was known for its variety of fish such as prawns, *halwa*, *rawas* and the famous Bombil or Bombay Duck, and in 1796 it became a cantonment area. In 1858, the Afghan Church was built. In 1873, the tramcars started running; two years hence, David Sassoon built the famous Sassoon Docks.

The causeway was constructed by the British East India Company during the tenure of Robert Grant, the Governor of Bombay in 1838, linking upper Colaba and the Old Woman's Island into one. Today, it is known as the Culture Square of Mumbai with its Portuguese and Victorian architecture merging elegantly. With art galleries, museums, cafés and upmarket retail showrooms as well as street-side kiosks, it is the Piccadilly of Mumbai.

The causeway of Mumbai is always buzzing. There are several eateries and watering holes. The place is full of people walking and window shopping as the entire road is dotted with shops selling a vast variety of goods. The small street-side stalls mainly cater to foreign tourists selling trinkets, curios, cotton casuals and fake pashmina. These colourful wares always made Jennifer feel less drab.

Some of the other guests at YMCA told Jennifer about the places to visit in the causeway. She went to Café Mondegar and Café Leopold several times to enjoy the lager there. Often she had the greasy yet tasty food at Olympia and Delhi Durbar. She especially loved the mutton *raan* at Abu Dana. Evenings in the causeway had the Arabs out, walking in their white robes, looking out for a little fun. Once Jenny even got propositioned by an Arab but she decided to ignore him.

Almost a fortnight into her stay, Jennifer began missing weed. She desperately needed some. She asked Philip quietly where she could get some. He directed her to a guy called Johnny who sold a lot of interesting 'stuff' at the causeway. 'He doesn't sell to anyone and everyone. Only if I recommend the person will he then sell. I'll tell you when and where to reach him,' Philip told her.

The next evening, Jennifer met Johnny with his green leather satchel—just as Philip had described him—next to Causeway Footwear near Delhi Durbar. The code sentence was, 'Hi, Dr Johnny. I am Philip's sister.' Every customer recommended by Philip was either his brother or sister depending on their gender. Only then did the short, dark Johnny with his salt-and-pepper hair open up. The prefix 'Dr' was a must.

'Yes Sister, what can I offer you?' Johnny asked in a funny English accent.

'Weed? Grass?' Jennifer enquired.

'Ah yes. Philip mentioned,' Johnny said as he handed her a small packet.

'How much?' Jennifer asked.

'Five hundred rupees. Not dollars,' Johnny laughed trying to be funny.

'Hey, you motherf***er,' Jennifer said quietly. 'You think I am stupid or what? I have been in the business for long', saying this, she put the packet in her sling bag as she pulled out a fifty rupee note and offered it to Johnny. Johnny looked aghast.

'No. No Sister. I cannot give you for fifty. You take for free then,' Johnny nodded. 'Okay. You give three hundred rupees.'

'Fifty,' Jennifer replied calmly.

'Okay. Hundred. Last price.'

'Nope. Fifty.' Johnny shrugged helplessly, unable to comprehend how to deal with this dark-skinned woman with an American accent. 'Besides Johnny, this is no good stuff,' Jennifer said after sniffing it. 'Next time you get me good weed and I will give you hundred rupees. Don't take me for a ch***a,' saying this Jennifer walked away leaving a zapped Johnny looking after her.

Ch***a was one of the first few cuss words Jennifer learnt in India. Besides her fortnight's stay in the city had taught her one lesson—the art of bargaining, an inherent Indian characteristic.

It was almost a month since Jennifer was in Mumbai, living in YMCA with Judy wiring the money for her stay through Western Union every week. And, YMCA was not cheap. The financial pressure was getting a bit too much for Judy, who worked in Chicago as a manager at the well-known accountant's firm, Seigal. Later she had to leave her well-paying job to look after Kadafi and Kassana. Judy's husband, Jesse Cobbs owned a Section A building in Chicago and was also its maintenance man. These apartments were occupied by low-income people, and the government provided the rent. Besides, the two of them were also responsible for Kadafi and Kassana, with their parents on the wrong side of the law and contributing nothing towards their upbringing. And now funding Jennifer's stay in a foreign land was getting a bit too much for Judy. Meanwhile, in Mumbai, Jennifer did try to do her bit by teaching English in a playschool in the neighbourhood, but she did not last there long enough to earn a month's salary. She could not get along with the other teachers and fought often. Judy asked her daughter-in-law to look out for cheaper options especially Christian homes for distressed people, which could be found in every corner of the world. Judy also asked Philip to look out for a cheaper lodging for Jennifer.

It was her last day at YMCA and Jennifer had grown fond of the place. 'Pack up and be ready by 7 p.m. My duty gets over and I have found you this very nice hostel for women in Colaba itself. On the main causeway. You will love it.' Philip assured Jennifer. After tipping Georgie Uncle, who did the housekeeping and hugging him goodbye, Jennifer moved on to her new abode.

Jennifer carried an overnighter, a better deal after her makeshift garbage-bag luggage holder. As she walked with Philip in her new Reeboks to a run-down building with wooden stairs leading to a small, shabby reception with Philip, Jennifer felt a little uncomfortable. A fat middle-aged woman in a maroon sari led her to a small dormitory. There were about six iron beds with small bedside lockers next to them. There were two such dormitories.

There were four girls chattering away in the dormitory she was led into. The chattering suddenly stopped as Jennifer came in with Philip and the lady, Mariamma. The girls looked at her with curiosity. All of them wore heavy make-up and wore bright red lipstick and bright sequined saris. They looked dressed for a party.

'Hello beauties,' Mariamma boomed. 'This is Jenny. From Amrica. She will stay with you. She is new. Please be nice to her. Show her around and explain everything to her. Help her with her needs. Got it.' Mariamma winked at the girls. 'Hey Radha. Come here and help Jenny.'

'Arrey Mariamma, from where you picked up this black imported maal [thing]?' one of the girls, Sheila, asked Mariamma crudely.

'Shut up you bitch.' Mariamma playfully admonished her.

Jennifer was almost in tears when Philip bade her goodbye. She almost followed him out but held herself back.

It was an awful night for Jennifer at the boarding house. The girls kept talking amongst themselves in the local language, and Jennifer felt she was being taunted at. They kept floating in and out through the night and Jenny could not sleep in peace. Besides, she was afraid she might get robbed if she slept too long or too deeply. She had a nagging feeling that something was amiss in this boarding house.

In the morning, Mariamma woke her up and showed her a common bath. After Jennifer brushed and bathed, Mariamma took her to a small dining room and gave her a buttered bun pao, the popular Bombay bun and kadak chai, sweetened strong milky tea.

'Single pao two rupees, double four. One cutting chai two rupees and full, four,' Mariamma rattled to Jennifer. 'If you want rice plate for lunch and dinner, twenty rupees for veg and thirty for non-veg. In veg you will get rice or chappatis with dal and vegetables and kachumber [a salad made with finely chopped onions, tomatoes, cucumber and green chillies]. In non-veg, one chicken dish extra. Sunday's fish, only bangda [Indian mackerel]. No prawns and pamphlet [pomfret, a much sought-after sea fish in Mumbai]. 'You don't want food here, you can go out and eat. But no bringing outside food here. Too messy,' Mariamma warned her. Jennifer wondered how could *anything* be messier than the shabby boarding house.

By evening, she felt she was in the wrong place. She would elicit odd looks from the nearby shop owners every time she entered or exited the boarding house. 'I felt like it resembled a whorehouse. Instinct told me it was.' That night her fears were justified. Mariamma got her a synthetic red sari with shiny sequins and a matching blouse and petticoat and asked Radha to drape it for Jennifer. When Jennifer asked why she was being dressed up like a Christmas tree, Radha told her she would be going to a party with them. 'What party?' she asked.

'Don't ask. We go for party every day. We do masti. You know masti? Fun? We have fun,' said Radha.

'Oh,' Jennifer said.

Meanwhile, Mariamma entered and on seeing Jennifer in a sari exclaimed, 'Hey you. You look sexy. Very sexy. Very good for business.'

'What business?' Jennifer asked suspiciously.

'Nice business. Sexy business for sexy girl. Good money,' Mariamma winked and laughed as Radha joined her. 'Okay I am going out Radha. You go down. Mister waiting down. You Jenny, come down when I call you. Okay.' Jennifer nodded.

The moment Radha and Mariamma left, Jennifer knew this boarding house was nothing but a front for prostitution. If she did not leave this place immediately, she would end up in the world's oldest profession. She put everything together hurriedly in her overnighter, picked up her sling and ran down the creaky stairs, evading the rest and into the Mumbai night in her garish red sari. She had difficulty walking in a sari, so she lifted it to her knees and started walking aimlessly avoiding the stares of passers-by and shopkeepers. She did not want to go back to YMCA, fearing Philip may send her back to the boarding house. She walked to the nearby Victoria Terminus (VT) railway station, a place she knew that always welcomed the homeless.

Jennifer walked faster, without turning back until the brightly lit Victorian facade of VT station appeared in front of her.

She had heard about VT, one of the busiest railway terminuses in the country. At last, she felt safe here amidst the milling crowd and bright lights. But she was not comfortable with the stares she elicited. The first thing she did was to change into her jeans and t-shirt from the garish red sari in one of the paid bathrooms at the station.

She knew women and children slept in VT station. She chose a place, where a lot of people were sleeping. Her immediate neighbour was an old beggar man, who slept a few feet away from her. She felt safer though she barely slept the night. She hoped that at least the cops would pick her up so she could sleep in jail, and wondered how an Indian jail would be like.

Jennifer spent two nights at VT station, barely sleeping for more than three or four hours in all. After the second night, she went back to the playschool to apologize and get her job back. 'But they wouldn't let me into the school as I was stinking. So, I went back to VT station, low, depressed, wondering what to do next,' Jennifer recollects.

She was hungry as she hadn't eaten anything since dinner and it was almost lunchtime. She strolled across and bought herself a cup of tea and a vada pao, the local equivalent of a hamburger, except this was vegetarian. Finding a quiet spot, she sat down with her bag by her side, hungrily biting into the vada pao when she noticed a familiar face smiling across the bench from her. She smiled back.

'Hi. I'm Patrick.'

'Hi Patrick,' Jennifer said with her mouth full.

'I have seen you before,' the thin, short and dark-skinned man smiled.

'Really? Maybe. Maybe not,' Jennifer tried to act nonchalant. She had seen him too. Perhaps, on the streets of the causeway. Perhaps, at Mondegar or Leopold's. She was not sure.

'You are the girl who has been deported from the US. Right?' Patrick asked. 'Jennifer. Right?'

Jennifer was zapped at this knowledge. 'How do you know, man? You have been following me or what?'

'Philip told me. I know him. I saw you with Johnny the peddler a few times. I saw you running out of the boarding house some days ago. I followed you here,' Patrick revealed. 'Philip tried to set you up there, didn't he?'

Jennifer gave him a hostile look. 'And what have you followed me for? You wanna take me back to that whorehouse? You better get this straight, I ain't going back there and if you bug me too much I will call the cops and have you arrested,' she said sternly.

'Please. Relax,' Patrick smiled. 'I have nothing to do with Philip and his settings. I have come here to help you. I am a social worker. I work with Home for the Homeless. It is also known as HTH. This is an international organization based out of Houston. I am heading the India branch from Mumbai.' Patrick showed her his card. Jennifer examined it thoroughly.

'Hmmm. So?' Jennifer wiped her mouth with the newspaper in which the snack was wrapped in, slowly sipping her tea from the plastic cup.

'You have nowhere to go. This place is not safe for you. There is a shelter home for women in Chembur, an hour's distance from here. It is run by Christian missionaries. It is called Women in Distress (WID). Let me talk to Father Fonseca and take you there,' Patrick said.

'And how do I trust you, Mr Patrick?' Jennifer asked cockily.

'Well, you have to take my word for it. You have to learn to trust me. I know it may be difficult, but that's that,' Patrick said as he showed her his ring finger with a gold band. 'I am a married man though my wife has gone to her native place at the moment. Besides, you don't have much choice, do you Jennifer?'

Jennifer nodded.

'Well I'll go with you. But, I'm warning you man, you try anything funny, you will regret it. I was jailed for aggravated felony back home...mugging and doing drugs and the works...' Jennifer broke off.

'Come. Let's go. Get your bag. It's already late,' Patrick said as he went about his business. He was used to dealing with cases worse than Jennifer.

Jennifer did not know why but she went along with Patrick. Her gut instincts told her she could trust him somehow. 'He gave me good vibes,' she says of the sprightly Indian Catholic social worker. He put her in a small hotel room in Colaba, and warned her not to open the door to anyone. Jennifer rested and the next morning Patrick joined her for breakfast as promised. Over breakfast, Jennifer told him everything about herself. Apart from her US deportation papers, the only other document she had was the affidavit showing Clarice D'Souza as her guardian during the time of her adoption.

Patrick immediately went about his research on Jennifer. They located the Kuan Yin Charitable Trust that Clarice ran in Colaba. But they were told by the security guard that Clarice was out of town. Patrick then took her to a priest in a church in Mahim and told him that Jennifer needed to be rescued. The priest mentioned Father Placito Fonseca, a Goan Catholic priest who knew Clarice, the woman who had processed Jennifer's adoption from the Kuan Yin adoption agency into the US. Jennifer and Patrick went to meet Father Fonseca, fondly known as Father Placee. They then found out that Clarice was in Kerala, holidaying with her children. Father Placee mentioned the shelter home for destitute women in Chembur which he had helped to establish. This home was run by sisters Jane and Teresa, amongst others.

Armed with a recommendation letter from Father Placee, Jennifer and Patrick took the Mumbai local from Colaba to Chembur and headed to Ashraya or Women in Distress (WID) on a cloudy afternoon.

6.

Thousands of children are adopted each year across geographical boundaries. Children mostly from developing and Third World countries are adopted into First World homes. The US adopts the largest number of children from other countries.

Inter-country adoptions are governed by laws of both countries— the one to which the child belongs as well as the one in which the adoptive parents live. There are two distinct inter-country adoption processes: the Hague Convention process and the non-Hague Convention process. But, before we get into the Hague Convention process, it is important to mention that the first international child rights adoption process was ratified by the United Nations (UN) in 1989, commonly known as the Child Rights Convention (CRC).

The UN ratified, 'Children for adoption should be kept within their geographical and economic milieu till they can move on and there should be certain uniform standards for children worldwide.' India signed the CRC in 1992.

The Hague Convention is a subsequent convention to the CRC, but is more detailed on the subject of inter-country adoptions. The preamble of Hague Adoption Convention process spells, 'Recognizing that the child...should grow up in a family environment, in an atmosphere of happiness, love and understanding.'

The US is party to the Hague Apostille Convention process on the protection of children and cooperation in respect to inter-country adoption since 1994. India is also a member of the Hague Convention.

In order to adopt Indian children into the US, there are certain criteria. To adopt children above three years, the adoptive parents should not be less than 25 years and not more than 55 years, or the couple should have a combined age of not more than 90 years. It is less in the case of younger children. Also parents should be medically fit with no contagious or terminal illnesses. India does not accept adoption by same sex couples and prefer married couples with at least five years of stable marriage before they file for adoption.

Since both the US and India are party to the Hague Convention, therefore both countries need to meet certain requirements as per the Convention Charter for adoption. These include choosing a US-accredited adoption service provider, being matched with a child by authorities in India, adopting and obtaining legal custody of the child in India, while simultaneously applying to the US immigration services for visa after fulfilling the eligibility requirements for adoption.

Indian children below the age of 18 are eligible for inter-country adoption only after being cleared by the Child Welfare Committees (CWC). The CWC is responsible for determining whether the child has been relinquished or abandoned or orphaned, and is ready for adoption.

The Central Adoption Resource Authority (CARA) is the adoption authority in India functioning under the Ministry of Women and Child Development. Once both the US and Indian authorities approve of the adoptive parents, then CARA may help in providing a child referral based on the review of a dossier between the adoptive parents and the needs of a specific child in India who could meet the requirements of that particular home. If the child is accepted, then CARA will communicate that to the service provider. It takes about 45 days to complete an inter-country adoption after it receives a No Objection Certificate (NOC) from CARA.

Ideally, India first tries to place an abandoned or relinquished child with an Indian family within the country, failing which they try to place the child with an ethnic family abroad and only as a last resort to a non-Indian family abroad. This is done so as not to displace an ethnic child and give him or her culture shock. However, this unsaid rule is flouted as adoption in non-Indian, especially American households, proves to be more lucrative than in Indian families.

If one goes by the requirements of CARA for inter-country adoptions, it can be quite daunting. It has laid out foolproof conditions so that children are not trafficked for illegal trade and activities in the name of adoption. Despite this, there are still a large number of children who end up in abusive homes. Instead of 'growing up in a family environment, in an atmosphere of happiness, love and understanding' as the Hague Convention specifies, they end up being abused and abandoned by the very family they are entrusted to.

7.

Located in the leafy suburbs of Chembur, Ashraya is a shelter for destitute and homeless women and their children. It was established in 1992 by Father Fonseca who was then running a home called Sneha Sadan in Andheri, managed by Jesuit priests.

Jennifer's first memory is of the church in the Ashraya complex. She recalled, 'The area was nice and clean with a lot of trees. It was a three-storeyed building with a parlour and offices on the ground floor. The first floor housed handicapped children, and a school for children was on the second floor. The third floor was home to about forty or fifty homeless women.'

'There were women from all communities and religion and some had babies. It was such a nightmare with the little babies as they cried through the night and disturbed our sleep. We all slept in a huge dorm and there was a separate room with lockers. We all had individual lockers to keep our stuff. The place was run by Father Placee, and Sisters Teresa and Jane looked after us. My favourite was Sister Jane, who was not only kind and compassionate but very understanding as far as I was concerned.'

'I was difficult to deal with and thoroughly spoilt as I was going through my own shit. Everyone got up at 7 a.m. and breakfast was served at 8.30 a.m. I did not follow the rules and since I did not eat breakfast, I got up as late as 9 a.m. I used to sleep late as I would be out on the terrace, smoking weed. It was my favourite place. The first thing I did on waking up was go to the terrace and start smoking!'

It was around this time that Justin was out on parole after serving three years. He had also 'dropped clean'—meaning, he was not doing drugs, and his urine tested negative for drugs. He called Jennifer every day. However, he was back to his business of selling dope and was making good money. He was very, very angry with her deportation and felt guilty at the same time.

With Justin out on parole, the children came to live with him as it was getting difficult for Judy to manage the children as well as her job. Despite his philandering ways and their many fights, Justin cared deeply for Jennifer, and not just because she was his wife or the mother of his children.

Every third day he wired four to five hundred dollars through Western Union, which Sister Jane would collect for her. This was a lot of money and still traumatized with her deportation and worried about her future, Jennifer decided on the best course of medication to allay her worries temporarily—retail therapy.

She frequented the shops along the causeway and sometimes nearer, on Bandra's Linking Road, buying herself clothes and shoes and a whole lot of weed. 'I loved wearing Reeboks and I bought myself two funky ones,' Jennifer says. 'Most of the girls were jealous of me because I would spend a lot on myself. They had never seen so much money. Also because of my American-accented English, I had an edge with the sisters. Some of the girls resented me.'

Even in the shelter home there was a hierarchy, a class system which Jennifer never experienced in the US. The girls who 'sucked up' to the sisters and were 'good to them' always got better food and fewer chores to do. Jennifer did not give in to such demands. Plus, she was a defiant girl who did not get along with most of the sycophantic girls. They were constantly provoking her. Once she had kept her clothes on the bench and gone for a bath in the cubicle of the common bathing room. On coming out she found her clothes scattered on the floor. She let it go the first time but when she realized it happened too often and only with her, she found out it was deliberately thrown on the floor by a Bangladeshi girl called Razia. One day, this girl picked up a fight with Jennifer. 'I beat the shit out of her. Sister Jane had to come and separate us. She tried to reason with me. After that I kept my distance from the residents.'

'I did not talk much but used my hand as a weapon whenever I felt the need to. Those bitches realized not to mess around with me much. In Battle Creek I had a soft heart. By the time I reached India I had become stone-hearted.'

Rina Jaiswal was perhaps the only girl with whom Jennifer could bond with in Ashraya. Rina was a quiet sort of a girl. A runaway at ten, Rina was the eldest of six siblings. She had left her mother and stepfather's home in Shillong, Meghalaya, because of her stepfather's verbal abuse. Not knowing where she was headed to, she boarded a Delhi-bound train but by a quirk of fate landed in Mumbai where she was put in a juvenile remand home. A year later she was shifted to Ashraya and stayed there for seven years till she moved to Ghansoli to start her own beauty business. From the beginning, Rina, who was three years older to Jennifer, was protective of her. 'Though Jenny was hyper and was always getting into fights, I treated her like my sister. Despite her harsh exterior, Jenny is a good friend and knows how to maintain true friendship,' says Rina. Theirs was a friendship that survived all weathers, and till date, in all her darkest hours, Rina stood by Jennifer.

Though the shelter provided a safety net for these distressed women, life was quite frugal with a monotonous routine. Meals were simple. Jennifer used Ashraya only as a safe zone to sleep. The rest of her time, she spent in Colaba or Bandra, watching movies, shopping and eating out. She bought herself a DVD player and watched movies. She had now built a new contact through one of the girls, Lakshmi, whose boyfriend Joshua supplied weed to her. Joshua was based in Bandra and Jennifer met him a couple of times a week and bought weed from him. 'His stuff was good, man. He sold good weed.' She once bought weed from a contact in Bandra, it gave her diarrhoea. Joshua sold drugs through this fat lady on Mount Mary, who used her kebab shop as a front for selling drugs.

She would stash the dope in her hostel locker till one of the girls tattled on her to Sister Jane. The Sister was initially upset at Jennifer for breaking her trust but when she realized Jennifer needed to smoke a controlled amount to keep her sanity, she counselled her not to go overboard and even gave her permission to smoke on the terrace.

'I just spent all my money living a good life and did not bother to save or even think of the future,' Jennifer says. Never did it occur to her that she would end up staying in this country for a long time. Deep down in her heart something told her that she would soon be back in the US with her husband and children. She believed Justin would find a way to get her back. She lived only in the present, spending money, getting high on weed and living a hedonistic life.

But this phase didn't last long. Barely a year into her deportation, Justin confessed to Jennifer one day that he was seeing a girl called Britney and he had moved in with her. Jennifer broke down. Sister Jane was a great source of strength for her at this time and helped Jennifer pray.

Kadafi and Kassana were sent back to live with Judy as Justin and Britney had a girl, Kiara out of wedlock. Soon the money from Justin became infrequent and finally one day it stopped altogether when Justin was locked up for dealing with cocaine.

This was one of the most difficult phases in Jennifer's life. Mentally, she was completely broken by Justin's confession. She was emotionally drained—bereft of her family, friends and country. Jennifer felt completely alienated. It began to dawn on her that she was not going back home anytime soon, and Justin's affair with Britney was the final nail in the coffin.

But despite everything, she somehow understood Justin's need for a female companion. Jennifer also needed a companion. Unfortunately for her, there were no males around in Ashraya. 'It was around this time I started dating a female resident. With Justin's betrayal I felt there was nobody for me. Since I had been away, I realized I wasn't able to connect with my kids that well. I felt totally alone in this world.'

'Initially this girl was very nice to me. She was kind, understanding and comforting—emotions I needed most at this time. Besides there was also a physical need, which we both were deprived of and needed. We started hanging out together more than ordinary friends would. And, finally I started dating her. The affair lasted for about six months or so, till she got married in Ashraya. I was heartbroken but felt happy for her. I realized this could not last forever. We both moved on.'

※

After Justin's imprisonment, Jennifer could not afford the little luxuries she had become used to in Chembur. Judy too was having a hard time running her house along with the additional charge of her grandchildren, and she was not able to send money to Jennifer on a regular basis. She told her daughter-in-law to find ways to fend for herself.

Jennifer got a job teaching English to young children in the house. There were no fixed timings but she taught them in the parlour for three hours a day on an average. She was paid a thousand rupees a month. The rest of the time she would hang around with friends she had made in Chembur. One of them owned a shop selling jeans and across the road from him was another guy Abdul who sold trinkets. Sometimes, they gave her some money for manning their shops while they went home for lunch. At other times they treated her to meals at home. Occasionally they even paid for her weed. 'They were friends so I enjoyed hanging around with them. Though I was in need of money, I did not ask them for it. It was a change from hanging around in the hostel. Also I was beginning to get a knack for selling goods and was doing rather well.'

'People would come to the stores just to see this dark Indian girl speaking American English. Some called me a dark American,' laughs Jennifer.

But after being spoilt by Justin's largesse of an average of sixty thousand rupees a week to fifteen hundred rupees a month, peanuts in comparison, Jennifer had to find other ways to sustain herself and her expensive habits. Besides, her meagre savings were diminishing rapidly.

Around this time Jennifer was offered the job of a governess to a little boy in Chembur.

Karen Sheikh was an English lady who was married to a Saudi businessman whose business dealings spread over continents. And like all sheikhs, Karen's husband too had several wives, Karen being one of many. Karen was deputed in Mumbai for some time as she taught in an international school. Her son Junaid was all of seven and Karen wanted a governess who would interact with him in English, give him his meals, help him with his homework, and take care of him until she returned from her school job. Jennifer took up the offer. Now, Jennifer would return to the shelter by evening. This was in 2010 and Jennifer was paid seven thousand rupees a month, peanuts by American standards but princely by Indian.

Slowly the work in the Sheikh household increased. From being a nanny and a governess at first, she ended up as a housemaid. Jennifer was made to do all the housework including cooking and cleaning, and was asked to stay on and not return to the hostel in the evenings. 'I had no time to myself. Unlike in the US there was no weekly off and I was on call 24/7,' recollects Jennifer.

'The class system was awful. I was made to feel like a lowly servant. I felt like a slave. I think it was slavery of the worst kind. Despite slavery being abolished in the US, the way the menials are treated in India, it is as if slavery still exists. I felt like a slave.'

Jennifer also got malaria while working for Karen but she refused to give her time off to recuperate. When Jennifer did not report to work due to weakness, Karen cut her salary. 'I had had enough and I decided to quit.'

8.

One of the first steps for prospective American adoptive parents, as per the Hague Convention, is to choose an accredited adoption service provider.

Americans for International Aid and Adoption (AIAA) is one of the oldest adoption agencies in the US dealing with inter-country adoptions.

AIAA was established during the Vietnam War in 1975 by Jodie and her husband Richard Darragh. Both Richard and Jodie worked with Eastern Airlines; Jodie as a flight hostess and Richard as ticket office manager. Both were from Marietta, Georgia.

AIAA was the first agency to be licensed for international adoption services in the state of Michigan and was Hague accredited in 2008. AIAA started out by relocating displaced children from the Vietnam and Korean wars to American homes in nearly all its fifty states. These babies were mainly 'war babies' who were orphaned or abandoned due to the wars, and were sometimes also 'Amerasians' (illegitimate children born of American soldiers and Asian women). Often without citizenship in their native lands and ignored by the country of their fathers, the lives of these children were tragic stories of endless political and cultural debates.

These Amerasian children were born to Korean and Vietnamese mothers and mostly American soldiers. Poor girls from the villages sometimes became 'wives', cooking and cleaning for soldiers during their posting, using the money to take care of not just themselves but also their families. When the American soldiers were transferred they often left their illegitimate children behind. Not recognized as Korean or Vietnamese, these children faced acute social stigma, and were educationally and economically deprived. This was especially the case if they were born of African-American men. Essentially, these children were stateless. Like most Asian societies, in Korea and Vietnam too, the father's lineage plays a key role in mapping out life opportunities.

Abandoned by their fathers, the future of these children was bleak.

Operation Babylift was the name given to the mass evacuation of children from erstwhile South Vietnam to the US and other countries such as Australia, France and Canada at the end of the Vietnam War in April 1975. President Ford then announced that the US would begin evacuating orphans out of erstwhile Saigon in a series of thirty planned flights. Organizations such as Jodie's AIAA and Cherie Clark's International Mission of Hope (IMH) were formed to help in the 'Babylifts'.

Taking advantage of her off days and discounted flight privileges as an airline employee, Jodie used to walk the backstreets of Seoul, Hanoi, Calcutta (present-day Kolkata) and other Third World countries in Asia and Africa to bring back abandoned children to the US and find adoptive homes.

Soon Jodie and Richard used their contacts to recruit stewardesses and their spouses from other airlines such as TWA, British Airways, Delta, Korean, North West and Orient who could use their discounted flight privileges to deliver medical supplies to Third World countries and bring back 'sick' children for treatment and 'orphans' for adoption. Soon the Darraghs built up a bank of more than 1,200 airline employees who ferried children from Asian and African countries into the US. They were known as 'escorts'.

One such escort, Suzanne Williams, who worked with Eastern Airlines in the early 1980s, said in an interview to *The Post* in 1982 that she had ferried over a hundred children from all over the world, including, Korea, Bogota, Nicaragua, Peru and India to the US. She was introduced to this work by a flight attendant on one of her holidays to London and ever since she felt 'her whole life changed. Now I help whenever and wherever I am needed. The love I give out I get back a million fold.'[5]

---

[5] Allan Zullo, 'Susan Williams: An eager escort for US-bound orphans'. Available at <https://www.csmonitor.com/1982/0322/032211.html> Accessed on 10 November 2019.

'We have many dedicated members,' admitted Jodie Darragh in the same interview. 'In a six-month period over a 150 AIAA volunteers made more than ten trips each to escort these unfortunate children and to help them get a better life.'

According to Jeannie Labels, a high school dropout from Miami who joined the Eastern Airlines, decided to look for a 'higher purpose' in life as she was at a 'loose end' and decided to volunteer with AIAA. She was immediately sent on a voluntary mission to Korea and on these trips she delivered clothing and other donations to orphanages in the countryside. On several trips she took a bus up to Father Keane's St Vincent's Home for Amerasian Children in Bu-Pyung, just outside of Inchon, and sometimes stayed over at the orphanage to get to know the children. Often she escorted some of these children to adoptive homes in the US.

Along with Jodie Darragh, Father Keane was instrumental in lobbying Congress for passage of the Amerasian Act in 1982. This Act allowed the 'war-lift children' to come to the US without their mothers or siblings. Since Vietnam objected, in 1987, Congress adopted the Amerasian Homecoming Act where mothers and immediate family members of Vietnamese Amerasians were allowed.

It was Senator Jeremiah Denton of Alabama, a friend of Jodie's and a former Vietnam POW, who was instrumental in passing the Amerasian Act to help legalize the 'baby war lifts'.

Who is Jodie Darragh?

We know she was a former Eastern Airline stewardess. She was close to Alabama Senator Jeremiah Denton. She flew mercy missions to Indochina and helped in the 'war baby lifts' to American homes with the help of other airline employees. She founded the AIAA. With help from Senator Denton, she lobbied for the Amerasian Act and the Homecoming Act in 1982 and 1987, respectively.

Jody Darragh also changed the spelling of her name from Jody to Jodie.

In a *People's* magazine interview in 1974, Jodie then 29 and Richard, 35, said they married in 1971. It was since then that the Darraghs used their travel privileges to ferry children from Korea, Vietnam and other Asian countries into US homes. It started with their first trip to an orphanage in Anloc near Saigon, and ever since the Darraghs became a team, with Richard or 'Dick', fastening bassinets to the plane's bulkhead, while Jodie mixed formula on a hot plate. They spent all their free time ferrying children as young as five months to eleven years old to the West.

Later, the Darraghs also adopted a two-year-old Vietnamese girl as Jodie was unable to bear children. The Darraghs were initially in constant touch with the children they helped, sometimes making several phone calls a night from their home in Marietta. Soon however, ferrying children became a bigger and more organized affair with many others joining them in their activities. When it became too much for the Darraghs to handle on their own, they formed the AIAA.

Like Jodie, there was another American lady called Cherie Clark who played a key role in Operation Babylift.

Cherie was born in a small town Peru in Indiana, and grew up to become a nurse. In the early 1970s, Cherie volunteered to help abandoned and orphaned children in Vietnam by nursing and looking after them. She was one of the key people who worked in Operation Babylift, an emergency evacuation of two thousand babies from Vietnam, and the only woman to be evacuated twice from there. In April 1975, she became famous for escaping from the country with a plane filled with babies after dodging rocket attacks to escape from Saigon's Tan Son Nhut airport. Her heroic exploits and early life can be read in her book *After Sorrow Comes Joy*.[6]

---

[6]Cherie Clark, *After Sorrow Comes Joy*, Lawrence & Thomas Publishing House, 2000.

Cherie founded IMH along with some adoptive parents united in a desire to bring hope to orphans in Vietnam, and to secure for them better homes outside the country. IMH is also known as the Cherie Clark Foundation today.

In 1975, Cherie travelled to India on the invitation of Mother Teresa's Missionaries of Charity, headquartered in Kolkata, to help in their childcare unit in West Bengal. For the next decade or so, Cherie stayed in India and helped build one of the finest child-care centres outside the US. Abandoned children, babies born in prisons, and those born of unwed mothers were all looked after and sent to school until suitable adoptive homes were found for them. Most of these children were sent to the US for adoption. Much later in 1988, Cherie returned to Vietnam where she set up orphanages and child-care centres including the one at Mai Lai where American troupes committed the worst atrocities.

Since both Jodie and Cherie worked in similar areas and situations, it was but obvious the two should meet. And they did.

They first met during Operation Babylift in Vietnam where Cherie supplied abandoned Vietnamese babies and Jodie used her airline privileges and networking skills to ferry these children to the US. Later their areas of supplying babies expanded to other Third World countries such as India, Bangladesh, Sri Lanka, Nepal, Korea and other African and Asian countries.

When Cherie returned to Vietnam in the late 1980s, Mary Graves, another social worker of Love the Children along with Jodie Darragh, carried on sending medical supplies to Vietnam and other Third World countries, and continued bringing in abandoned and orphaned children from these countries into the US.

9.

It was nearly two years at Ashraya and Jennifer's difficult behaviour was becoming a matter of grave concern at the home. Though Sister Jane was sympathetic towards her, she was becoming a handful for the rest of the residents.

Apart from smoking weed and beating up fellow residents, she refused to comply with the rules and was often abusive. To Jennifer, Ashraya was just a stopover before she made it back to the US. Unfortunately, after a year-and-a-half later, Jennifer realized that the stopover was going to be endless. She was claustrophobic and edgy, and this edginess was manifested in her abusive acts towards the rest of the residents.

Father Placee then decided to bring in a young social worker, Sangeeta Punekar to counsel Jennifer. Sangeeta tried to help Jennifer with her problems, and spoke with her about what she could to do with her life in India since returning to the US seemed a distant dream.

According to Jennifer, Sangeeta was not sympathetic to her problems and was unable to comprehend them wholly. 'I didn't get along with her,' says Jennifer. 'She did not understand me. All she was interested in was using me as a case study.'

Sangeeta was working on a project with Save the Children when she was handed over Jennifer's case by Sister Jane. 'Initially I found it a little strange. Jennifer could be lucid at times and at other times completely clamped up but she had clear memories of being in a house till the age of five with her parents and an older brother and definitely not an orphan as she was later made to believe. In fact, she also remembered being left in some sort of a shelter with other children and made to study and sleep on the floor as she would be frequently bed-wetting. This shelter as we know is part of the Kuan Yin Charitable Trust and was in Byculla.'

'For the longest time Jennifer did not have the confidence to admit that she was violated. She was picked up for felony post 9/11 and was deported soon after it was found that her papers were not in order. The stupidest thing the Indian government did was to accept her. It was the US government's responsibility to process her papers at the time of adoption, and they would have done that had we refused to accept her here.'

What Sangeeta goes on to enumerate about inter-country adoption is that though there are many Indian families wanting to adopt, we are very keen to appease the 'big fat white man', and thereby clearly going against the UN Convention. And while living in a picture postcard American home may seem dream-like, it remains just that because adjusting to a different culture can be very painful. A lot of pain and distress goes into inter-country adoption.

'In India, grabbing a child out of the arms of a poor mother is the easiest thing to do,' says Sangeeta. And, Clarice D'Souza did exactly that according to her. 'She did not tell the absolute truth to AIAA while she was processing Jennifer's papers. She lied in court to procure a false abandonment certificate, claiming Jennifer's parents were dead though she knew very well that they were alive. She also misled her parents into believing that she was sending Jennifer to the US for education instead of saying that she was being taken away for adoption. And mind you [she did] all without her mother's knowledge. Clarice did all this for monetary gain.'

'Well, that is the sad truth about inter-country adoptions from India. No one looks at the child's future; they look at their personal profits. There are some horrific stories to how children are forcibly snatched from perfectly happy homes and sent for adoption. How perfectly normal children are maimed for life to cater to religious whims and fancies. I was horrified when an NGO told me that sometimes we have to cut the child's arms to send the child abroad!'

Around this time, following Sangeeta's advice, Jennifer decided she needed a passport to be able to work in India. In order to do this, she needed to track her biological parents who were Indian. 'More than getting a passport, I was very very curious about my biological parents. I was very keen to locate them,' says Jennifer.

It was with the help of her adoption papers that Sangeeta decided the best way to track her biological parents. For this, they needed to get in touch with Clarice who oversaw the orphanage run by the Kuan Yin Charitable Trust. It was the same orphanage where Jennifer was placed as a six-year-old by her mother—believing it to be a safe zone for her education—and the same institution from where she was sent for adoption in the US.

'The only clue I had to locating my biological parents was a scrap of paper saying that Clarice D'Souza was my guardian,' recounts Jennifer. 'Sangeeta, with the help of Father Placee, got in touch with Clarice D'Souza. We decided to go and meet her. Sangeeta also introduced me to her friend Pradeep Havnur, a lawyer, who set up a meeting with Clarice.'

'On my first meeting with Pradeep, I immediately took a liking to him. He gave me good vibes like Patrick and my instinct told me I could trust him. Besides he was not as bossy as Sangeeta. The three of us went to meet Clarice.'

※

Originally from Dharwar in Karnataka, Pradeep is a graduate from the Government Law College, Mumbai, and a practising lawyer at the Bombay High Court since 1991. He mainly deals with human rights issues.

In 2004, Pradeep along with Father Placee and Sangeeta formed the Advait Foundation which deals with rehabilitating sexually abused rescued children. It was Sangeeta and Father Placee who brought in Pradeep to help out Jennifer.

'The first time I met Jennifer was in 2008 in Ashraya in Chembur.

Jennifer bummed a cigarette from me and we went out and had a smoke together. This was fifteen minutes before our meeting with Clarice D'Souza. Hearing her story of having left two small children behind and thrown out of a country after having lived there for twenty years, my heart went out to her. I felt if there was any person on this planet who needed unconditional help, it was Jennifer and it was then that I resolved to do everything I could to help her return to the US,' reminisces Pradeep.

'When the frail, dark Clarice came out, she was as stubborn as a mule. She refused to divulge the whereabouts of Jennifer's biological parents.'

'Your parents told me never to reveal their identity to you,' Clarice seemed dodgy.

'But isn't it your duty to have overseen that Jennifer's papers were processed in the US once you sent her there?' Pradeep asked. Clarice seemed to be ducking all questions. All she kept repeating was that Jennifer's mother always wanted her to go abroad. However, Pradeep knew only too well because inter-country adoption was a subject which interested him greatly. 'Despite there being judgement after judgement by the Supreme Court on this, a child [is] never given up willingly for adoption. It [is] always under coercion and duress.'

'Fraudulent papers are made by adoptive agencies when there is a complete loss of contact between parents and their children and the agencies. It is then that these agencies make false affidavits and abandonment certificates. In order to hoodwink the authorities, money is normally pumped into these agencies in the form of donations and not for adoption. To change the records of a stolen car is more difficult than a stolen child,' says Pradeep after his extensive study in the field.

Clarice's stubbornness to reveal Jennifer's biological parents and take responsibility for her sorry plight angered Pradeep who threatened her with a criminal lawsuit. 'I will see you in court Ma'am, though right now I feel like pulling out your nails one at a time to make you feel the pain that Jennifer is feeling at the moment,' raged Pradeep, seething with fury.

Clarice was shaken but Jennifer's reaction melted Pradeep's heart, 'I like you, man. I like you,' she told Pradeep.

Pradeep was also the founder member of ACT, the organization that played a major part in rehabilitating Jennifer's life. While Pradeep took up her case in the courts, fighting to send Jennifer back into the US, Arun was one of the key ACT activists, who sourced all the research and paperwork for the matter. Meanwhile, Anjali Pawar, a social worker associated with ACT tried to be around Jennifer and help her trace her family and biological parents.

10.

Child trafficking was always a profitable trade but with the US government legalizing the 'babylifts', it actually became a legalized profitable trade that opened up opportunities of supplying Third World orphans to First World homes under the garb of non-profit organizations (NPOs).

The whole scheme of this operation is seldom based on love and humanity, but more on profitability as per demand and supply. As demand for babies increased in First World countries, it began to be met by supply from the Third World and poorer nations. However, such supplies did not always follow the rule books.

Allegedly, out of the hundred babies sent out for adoption to 'loving and happy homes' as specified in the Hague Apostille, barely a third find their way to such homes. Though some may end up in adoptive homes, seldom are they 'happy' or 'loved' there. Children are often sexually abused and mistreated. A third of the hundred end up as cheap child labour while the rest of them find themselves as organ donors and subjects of medical research.

This is horrific but true. This is the reality of inter-country adoption.

※

On 22 August 1982, the London tabloid *The Mail on Sunday*, a sister publication of *The Daily Mail*, published a story accusing Jodi Darragh's AIAA of using airlines privileges to 'sell infants to American families for $3,480 each'. Further, they also alleged that most of the children were not really orphans but were forcibly bought from their poor and illiterate parents for pittance and sold at high and profitable rates to rich American homes. The London tabloid went on to say that organizations sold infants from Calcutta, Saigon and slums from other Asian cities. These children were carried on British Airways, Trans World Airlines (TWA) and other airlines by off-duty attendants.

Jodie responded to the allegation on 23 August 1982 in a piece published in the *Chicago Tribune* denying that the infants were being sold for money. 'Our group is a non-profit organization run by volunteers and they escort the children to their new homes for the joy of escorting. They are reimbursed only for their expenses,' Jodie had told the *Chicago Tribune*.

But, the article in *The Mail on Sunday* not only exposed the tip of the iceberg in the irregularities in inter-country adoptions but also alerted the airlines and government agencies. British Airways and some others immediately suspended flights involving children. That one expose had proved very costly for Darragh who insisted, 'We are ruined now. Our reputation is down the tubes.'

Meanwhile, the impact of this article reached as far as Calcutta where the Indian government decided to probe into the workings of Cherie Clark's children shelter there, and halted legal adoptions of Indian children by American couples for a while. In fact, Clark's association with Mother Teresa also brought the activities of the Missionaries of Charity under the scanner. The mission was allegedly getting international funds in the form of donations in lieu of services provided in the guise of charity.⁷

❦

As a schoolgirl, growing up in Calcutta and studying in a convent run by sisters of Mother Teresa's Order, she was more than Mother Superior to me. In fact, she was saint-like. Even the average non-Christian Bengali felt that way. Yet, as my memory clearly serves me, there was a series of newspaper articles alleging that the Missionaries of Charity headed by Mother Teresa, forcibly took poor children, converted them to Christianity and sent them abroad as child labour.⁸ There was much hue and cry about a girl child allegedly kept in the Missionaries of Charity home in Calcutta for some time without her mother's consent before she was slyly trafficked to Germany.

For a while, the average Bengali's ire was evident as many doubts and aspersions were cast upon her social work. 'It is all to make money. Social work is only to hoodwink us,' I remember an uncle being voluble on this subject. Such were the opinions of many during their evening discussions or *adda*.

As many as thirty infants who were due to fly out to adoptive homes, were held back. While Darragh cried out the baby sale racket as 'garbage' from New York, Clark insisted from Calcutta that it was 'a bunch of lies' and 'we're a bunch of people down here who care about children'.

Nevertheless, the article published in *The Mail on Sunday* did raise

---

⁷Scott Neuman, 'Late Mother Teresa's Order investigated for child trafficking In India', NPR, 17 Jul 2018. Available at <https://www.npr.org/2018/07/17/629681931/late-mother-teresas-order-investigated-for-child-trafficking-in-india> Accessed on 4 Nov 2019.
⁸Walter Wuellenweber, 'Mother Teresa: Where are her millions?' Deesha, September 1998. Available at <https://deeshaa.org/wuellenweber-where-are-her-millions/> Accessed on 4 Nov 2019.

a whole lot of uncomfortable questions that plagued inter-country adoptions.

Geeta Ramaswamy, the noted author of *India Stinking: Manual Scavengers in Andhra Pradesh*,[9] a book on the manual scavengers of Andhra Pradesh and their work, has also co-authored a book on the Lambada community of Andhra titled *Lambadas: A Community Besieged*.[10] Originally a nomadic tribe with caravan traders, the members of this community ended up engaging in criminal activities when caravan trading was hampered under the Nizams' rule. They acquired the label of being a 'criminal community'. According to Ramaswamy, a Lambada child's rate in the international market was anything between ₹5 lakh to ₹25 lakh. This was over a decade ago. Today, it is almost double. Her book is one of the few important sources that look into the pricing of children for trade.

In Canada too in the 1970s, a group of four Canadian mothers adopted between themselves fifty orphans from Bangladesh, Cambodia and Vietnam and put up hundred more for adoption.[11] These women who came to be known as the 'maverick mothers' claimed it was a sense of 'maternal internationalism' which inspired them. However, when the authorities were not convinced with their intentions, their 'humanitarian work' came under much scrutiny.

---

[9]Geeta Ramaswamy, *India Stinking: Manual Scavengers in Andhra Pradesh*, Navayana Publishers, 2011.
[10]Geeta Ramaswamy, *Lambadas: A Community Besieged*, UNICEF, 2002.
[11]Tarah Brookfield, 'Maverick Mothers and mercy flights: Canada's controversial introduction to international adoption', Erudit, 28 May 2009. Available at <https://www.erudit.org/en/journals/jcha/2008-v19-n1-jcha3094/037436ar/> Accessed on 6 Nov 2019.

11.

Anjali Pawar was a young activist and law student from Pune when Jennifer met her. Anjali was a member of ACT, along with Pradeep Havnur, Arun Dohle and Roelie Post. Jennifer was first referred to her by Sangeeta. 'When I first met Jennifer she was a very disturbed soul. It was understandable. She was moody and kept crying and was constantly getting into trouble and fights. It was extremely difficult for Sangeeta and me to handle her because she was always abusing us and using bad words. She called me a "b**ch" and no one had called me that before. I would have whacked the person but knowing Jennifer's situation, I let that go. Her behaviour was very American, very alien,' says Anjali.

Despite her difficult behaviour, Jennifer hung around in Anjali's place in Pune, 'smoking up and drinking'. Jennifer described Anjali as 'an okay b**ch'. But that is how Jennifer was—you are either a 'b**ch', or a 'motherf****er' or 'bh***ri'. When in generous mood, she would say 'man' or 'dude'.

Anjali further says, 'More alien was Jennifer herself as she had no documents to support herself. No passport, no birth certificate, no nothing. She was like an alien on this planet. It was then that Pradeep, Sangeeta and I decided to appeal for her case in the High Court. We also worked towards getting her a passport.'

Anjali and Jennifer also went to meet Clarice but she refused to help saying, 'she was under oath not to reveal her biological mother'. Finally, they managed to get some documents from her American lawyers, James Marshall and Karyn Schiller.

'There was a baptismal certificate in the documents though the writing was not clear,' says Anjali. 'There was a mention of Wilma and Bosco and a Fatima Church in Ambernath. I asked a friend to check it out and she confirmed the existence of the Church. This was much before the Google days.'

Much later, on 11 February 2011, Jennifer Edgell Haynes finally got her Indian passport and with that, a nationality. When she entered the country in 2008 she was totally confused. She was in a limbo. After making twenty or thirty trips to the passport office and 'shedding many tears for this document', and with the help received from Father Placee, Sangeeta and others along the way, Jennifer's finally received her most prized possession—her passport.

'Getting her passport was the biggest challenge as there was not a shred of paper or document to start with', recollects Sangeeta. 'Since she did not have any papers she was non-existent. Both in India and the US. So, I told the officials if she is technically not born and does not exist, tell me how do we bury her? She needed a passport in order to earn an honest living or she would end up as a prostitute. Besides, one could not penalize her for life because her papers were not right for no fault of hers!'

In an interview with Mayura Janwalkar in *The Indian Express* in September 2011, Jennifer admitted, 'It feels good to know where you come from. I was totally confused when I first got here, but I know now that I am Indian. However, the American in me has not withered away. I have a passport but I am still very far from seeing my children.'

'I am now trying to adjust to Indian ways and move on. I survived by doing odd jobs but now with a passport I am a little more hopeful. Hopeful of getting a better job and hopeful of visiting my children and my family back in Michigan.'

Armed with her new document and a new identity and nationality, Jennifer moved out of the home in Chembur. She moved in with a friend Rina from Ashraya, in Ghansoli near Thane. Rina had started her own beauty salon with the help of Father Placee and Sister Jane a few months back. Jennifer joined a call centre in the neighbouring Airoli called Neural IT.

And, so started a new innings in the Indian chapter of Jennifer's life.

※

One bright summer morning, Anjali and Jennifer took the train to Ambernath, a small hamlet in Thane, nearly 100 km outside of Mumbai. Ambernath literally means 'Sky Lord', and is the site of an old Shaivaite temple dedicated to Lord Shiva dating back to AD 1060.

Jennifer had no recollection of her childhood or Ambernath. 'All I remember was [that] it was very far from Mumbai. When I first saw Fatima's Church with a priest standing in front in his habit, I suddenly felt homesick for Battle Creek. It all looked so pretty.'

Anjali and Jennifer went up to the priest, 'Father, I am looking for a parishioner', Anjali said. 'Can you please help me?'

'Sure,' the smart, young man replied. 'Who is it?'

Anjali noticed that there was a huge crowd gathered outside the Church and all were gathered in front of a casket. 'Someone died, Father?' Anjali asked.

'Yes,' replied the priest. 'One of our oldest parishioners. Judy Gomes. She was ailing. 91 years. Her children have come from Cochin. Yes, so who was it you were looking for?'

'Bosco Francis? Wilma Francis?' Anjali asked as she showed the priest the baptismal certificate.

'No. Never heard of them. I don't think they belong to this parish...I am sure of that,' the priest replied.

'Just look here Father...maybe the other names here...the godparents...Toto Middleton, godfather? Or, Gunnie Charles, godmother? Do you know them?' The priest nodded in the negative. Anjali looked lost but was not one to give up easily. She looked at Jennifer's face. The latter was ready to burst into tears. This was the one last hope Jennifer had harboured to find her biological parents, and this too seemed to be slipping away.

Suddenly a short, grey-haired chubby old man came from behind the priest and said, 'Hey. Bosco Francis? Wilma Francis? I know that family.'

Anjali could not hold back her excitement as Jennifer's shiny skin crinkled in a smile. 'It was a sad time for the family of Judy Gomes but it was an excellent time for me as the whole congregation had gathered and someone or the other was bound to know of Jennifer's biological family in Ambernath,' Anjali said. She showed the chubby old gentleman the baptismal certificate.

'Oh my God! Pinky you have grown so big! Look,' he called out to an elderly lady, presumably his wife, 'Come here *na*...Margaret. See who is here? Wilma's daughter. Pinky. From Amrica. She has come all the way from Amrica. And see how big and tall she has become.' Saying this he hugged the fairly tall and robust Anjali.

'Shh. Quiet.' Margaret said as she came and hugged Anjali. 'My, my...Wilma's daughter. Pinky you have become so big. Bigger than your father and brother. Good food in Amrica *na*...that is why you are big and strong.'

'Sorry,' Anjali said awkwardly. 'I am not...'

'When you came from Amrica?' Margaret cut her short. 'You should have come a little early *na*...'

'Aunty, I am not Pinky. She is Pinky,' Anjali said pointing at Jennifer. 'She is Wilma's daughter...'

'Oh. Accha.' Margaret mumbled. 'I...but, of course. You look so much like Christopher. She looks like Christopher *na* Joel...Just like her brother.' The chubby Joel nodded.

'Oh. So you know my mother and my father,' Jennifer looked excited. 'Where are they? Where do they live?'

'There she is. There is Wilma. There is your mother,' Joel said as he pointed to the graveyard adjoining the Church. 'You are late my child. Wilma died five years ago.' A few moments of silence followed as Jennifer swallowed her sorrow and went to the grave of her 'real mother' Wilma, and sat looking at the gravestone. While Jennifer sat alone in silence, Joel and Margaret told Anjali about Bosco and

Wilma. How Bosco and Wilma fought because of Bosco's alcoholism and how Wilma decided to put Pinky in a boarding so that she got a good education. But, when Wilma returned to the boarding school to meet Pinky they informed her that her daughter had been selected to study in the US, and she never saw her after that. Over the years, Wilma could not keep track of her daughter's progress as the boarding school (Kuan Yin) had closed down. Wilma believed that her daughter would return one day with lots of money, and make her old age comfortable. But that never happened as Wilma died of ill health, heartbroken at not being able to see her daughter.

Jennifer was deported in 2008 while Wilma died in 2006. The cause for her death remains a mystery though rumours have it was due to a venereal disease. Her brother Christopher however says she died of a stomach tumour.

'Joel was an old parishioner and an old family friend of the Francises. So the spiel Clarice gave about being sworn under oath is pure bullshit. Jennifer was a kidnapped child, snatched away from her parents under lies,' said Anjali.

It was the following Wednesday that Jennifer met up with Joel at the Ambernath station who promised to take her to meet her brother. Sister Jane had accompanied Jennifer, and they all had a little lunch of vada pao at a small stall by the station. They then took an auto rickshaw and went to her brother's little hut.

'Hi Madhuri,' Joel called out to a slim, tall young woman in a sari. 'Christopher *kuthey*? Where is your husband?'

'He has gone to work, Uncle. Why?' Madhuri immediately covered her head with the sari pallu.

'Then call him from work. Now. See who has come, Madhuri? Christopher's sister from Amrica. Pinky. Your nanad…sister-in-law,' Joel spoke as the shy Madhuri folded her hands in front of Jennifer in a namaste. Jennifer hugged her. Then she saw a small boy slung in a cloth tied to two bamboo sticks, an apology for a crib. 'Your nephew,' Joel explained. 'Christopher's son.'

Madhuri went to call her husband and Jennifer looked around the shabby little hut with its peeling paint. She was horrified to see the stark poverty written all over the hut and its inhabitants. Even the jail room in Calhoun County looked better than this. On the wall, she saw, among other photographs, a smiling coloured photograph of a pretty woman with short hair. This must be her mother, she thought to herself. As if reading her mind Joel announced, 'Pinky, that is Wilma…'

Her eyes blurred as she heard Joel rattle on, 'And that is Christopher and…'

Ten minutes later Christopher came in. 'Pinky!'

Jennifer turned around. He came and hugged and kissed her. Jennifer repeated like a zombie. With no feelings. 'I had no feelings for him,' she recollected. 'But when I looked at him, I knew he was my brother. He was a mirror image of me. We looked exactly alike. There was no denying he was my brother.'

Initially, Jennifer felt Christopher resented her because he thought she would now try and stake her claim on his little hut. Christopher of course denies having any such thoughts. 'I was just happy to see my little sister after all these years,' is what Christopher says of their first meeting.

'My mind was not there with my biological family though I was there physically. The reason was I was in a foul mood as my iPod which Justin had sent me was stolen in Ashraya and, man! I was really pissed,' Jennifer said.

Jennifer then noticed a skinny old man, shabbily dressed standing at a distance, staring at her.

'Who's he?' Jennifer asked.

'He is your father,' Joel said.

'Oh,' is all Jennifer had to say.

There was awkwardness between father and daughter after all

these years. Jennifer took a couple of photographs with her newly discovered family. There wasn't much verbal interaction because of the language barrier. Her family spoke mainly Marathi while she spoke only English.

'I had no feelings. No emotions. I was just curious. All feelings were dormant. I was totally f*cked up and I felt then that had they not given me away, at least I would have been f*cked up here,' was all Jennifer remembers of her first meeting with her brother and father.

12.

ACT is an international non-government organization (NGO) focusing on the prevention of child trafficking for inter-country adoptions. It was founded in 2010 by two like-minded individuals, Roelie Post and Arun Dohle. If Roelie and Arun had their way, inter-country adoption would disappear five years from now.

However, profits garnered from inter-country adoptions run into billions of dollars and some of the most powerful people and organizations from numerous fields—politics, education, government, royalty and even religion—are involved in this thriving trade. Despite the strong mafia involved, ACT claims that in its five years of existence its relentless efforts have led to a reduction in inter-country adoptions worldwide by 65 per cent. This has been achieved by seriously risking the lives of its team members.

Fifty-five-year-old Roelie has been a European Union (EU) official for twenty years, of which she was responsible for overseeing foreign adoptions from Romania for six years between 1999 and 2005. It was during her EU days that she stumbled across the case of Marineta Ciofu, an illiterate, poor Romanian single mother whose daughter was illegally trafficked from a children's shelter without her permission. It was ten years later that Marineta found out that her daughter had been adopted by an American family. The transaction was recorded without her knowledge. This bears a striking resemblance to Jennifer Haynes' case where Jennifer's adoption was transacted without her mother Wilma's knowledge, with Clarice and the adoption agencies taking advantage of her illiteracy and poverty.

This set Roelie thinking. According to her, 'Poverty is no reason to take children away. Poverty is not a disease and international adoption is not the cure.' But, the business was lucrative and the mafia, strong. A rough estimate indicates that in the decade after Communist rule in Romania, 30,000 children were sent to adoptive homes, mainly in the US, at the rate of $30,000 per child making it a whopping US$900 million trade. This is not an exaggerated figure. 'The US is one of the worst countries for adopted children from abroad,' says Roelie, citing the case of the three-year-old Russian boy who died in his American adoptive home due to excessive beatings. Through her persistent lobbying against international adoption, she was, amongst several others, able to bring about the moratorium against foreign adoptions in 2001 in Romania. 'Today, there are over 43,000 children in state childcare homes and for every child there are at least two Romanian couples willing to adopt.'

Given this example, and taking our huge population into consideration, if all children were sent to Indian homes, there would hardly be any left to 'export abroad'! But, then you need more Roelie Posts and Arun Dohles to continue with their single-minded passion despite all bureaucratic influences and child mafia threats. What is amazing is that while working in the EU, Roelie continued to run ACT, which in principal was against the EU policy!

Roelie has been ably assisted from the beginning by Arun, who shares the same passion as her regarding inter-country adoption. In his early forties, Arun was born in India but adopted by a German family in 1973. 'Fortunately for me, my adoptive family was very nice. I grew up in Aachen and had a happy childhood, unlike most cases of adoptive children I deal with now.' What brought Roelie and Arun together is this common goal of abolishing foreign adoption. Arun admits it is extreme but 'very achievable as the world of adoptions is a world without real controls'.

Apart from Roelie and Arun, ACT also has Anjali and Catherine Wagner as key activist members as well as an international panel of lawyers such as Dr Eric Agstner, Pradeep Havnur and Bianka Stege, who are experts in inter-country adoption laws.

Another area that ACT focuses on is to help connect these trafficked adoptees with their biological parents or kin with the help of local NGOs. This is part of their Parents Assistance Project (PAP). Since most of the adoptees are trafficked due to the poverty of their parents, there is no way for them to get in touch with their 'kidnapped children' as most of them are illiterate, living below the poverty line in remote regions. With the help of the goodwill of local NGOs, many children adopted abroad have been able to trace their biological parents despite having little evidence by way of papers.

Take the example of Anisha, whose mother could not pay the hospital bill when she was born and so she was sent to a German home without her mother's knowledge. ACT helped Anisha trace her mother after 28 years. Or Betty, who was returned to her Ethiopian parents from her Danish adoptive home with ACT's help. Or, the time when Nagarani and Karthivel complained of their minor son being kidnapped, it was ACT which traced their son to a Netherlands adoptive home via a Malaysian Agency through Indian abductors. ACT also helped Fatima and her husband Salya travel to Australia to meet up with their 16-year-old daughter who was snatched away from them from the streets of Chennai when she was two. Sadly, the daughter, Zabeen, refused to meet her biological parents as they were 'very poor' and would 'embarrass' her.

However, one of the most intriguing cases of ACT under its PAP was retracing Arun's biological mother. Arun was two months old when he was adopted by a German couple, Michael and Gertrude Dohle. He had a happy childhood at Aachen but during his teenage years, he resented his 'different look' from his peers. It led him to believe he was abducted from his biological parents and was curious to trace them. He first visited India as a 20-year-old and several visits later, and with legal help from Pradeep and Anjali, Arun was able to meet his biological mother after almost four decades in 2010. All his fears and apprehensions were put to rest after he was told that since he was conceived out of wedlock (a taboo in Indian society), his mother surrendered him soon after birth to the Kusumbai Motichand Sevagram in Pune. His mother married later in life.

Closer home, it was ACT with the help of Anjali and Jennifer's old, faded and tattered baptismal certificate that she was able to locate her biological father and brother in the outskirts of Mumbai in Ambernath. She was also able to find out that Jennifer's mother never gave her up for adoption; instead she was snatched away from her mother, in other words, 'kidnapped' and then 'trafficked' out of the country.

13.

Child trafficking is a lucrative business worldwide. It is an ancient racket from the time of Christ with some of the most powerful men and women belonging to a secret sect. It is believed to have members from European and Asian royalty, bankers, hedge fund owners, senators, political heads and Ivy League professors as well as top professionals such as scientists, sports and film personalities.

Therefore to crack this organization is near impossible. The blatant disregard for inter-country adoption laws is possible because some of the richest organizations in the world run by very powerful people are behind child trafficking.

This powerful, elite group has survived through generations from the time of Christ. It is a secret organization which no one dares name but all know exists. This is the Illuminati.

Illuminati is an elite Mafioso and their reach is all-pervading and dangerous. Several NGOs including ACT, which have come out strongly against inter-country adoptions, have been threatened by them, and some social workers and activists have also mysteriously disappeared. Allegedly, this organization also has the tacit support of the Vatican.

To prove a point, as recently as 3 January 2015, there was a news item in British newspapers stating Prince Andrew's tryst with a 17-year-old minor 'sex slave', who was given to him by the American multi-millionaire Jeffrey Epstein.[12] Alan Dershowitz, a Harvard law professor and defence lawyer, was also allegedly involved. Here we find a millionaire, a brilliant lawyer, European royalty and a minor sex slave—all part of a transcontinental elite organization. Sounds almost like the highly secret organization, the Illuminati.

Some of the well-known Illuminati members allegedly include several US presidents as well as a former Secretary of State, who was once considered the CEO of the organization. Some members also apparently include some top Hollywood stars and closer home, a couple of Bollywood celebrities.

There is a Greek saying that a fish rots from the head downward and if this is to be believed then most political leaderships stink. According to some, allegedly every Western nation is run by a shadow government, which owes its loyalty to the previously mentioned

---

[12]Joanna Walters, 'Prince Andrew was an abuser, Epstein accuser says in TV interview', *The Guardian*, 20 September 2019. Available at <https://www.theguardian.com/uk-news/2019/sep/20/prince-andrew-abuser-claims-virginia-giuffre-tv-interview> Accessed on 6 Nov 2019.

secret organization. Most political leaders are chosen by their moral frailties, blackmail abilities and willingness to advance the sect's plan. Many are said to live a life that may include paedophilia, drugs, child pornography, satanic rituals and child sacrifices. They are given many opportunities to indulge in their vices, which mean obedience and loyalty in return. It does not matter which political party they belong to, as long as they serve the cause of this sect.

A curious example was the recent US elections. Donald Trump, a billionaire businessman with zero political experience managed to win the Presidential elections over a veteran politician, Hilary Clinton. This is despite Clinton reigning high in the popularity charts. Apparently, he was backed by the Illuminati, who are actually running a shadow government to the world's most powerful country knowing Trump's human frailties, and consequently having a major hold over the world's finance by controlling arms, drugs and the child-trafficking trade.

The chiefs of the sects or 'world shadow government' are given authority over particular regions. Most of them are descendants of an ancient dynastic bloodline, mostly royal. Some are plain rich. Money and bloodline are key points for membership. Drugs, prostitution, human and child trafficking are the biggest source of finance for this secret sect representing the New World Order programmes. Top officials from the Central Intelligence Agency (CIA), Federal Bureau of Investigation (FBI), Interpol, Coast Guard, and military and police are all allegedly involved to further the cause of the Illuminati. How much of this is real and how much fictitious is anybody's guess.

The current scenario in inter-country adoptions and child trafficking is very frightening. Drug cartels have moved on to human smuggling business and nothing pays as well as selling children.

Child sex trafficking earns about 32 billion dollars a year. One million go missing in a year in the US alone. Allegedly, there are 20–30 million child slaves used for sex magic and other perverse rituals sponsored by the Illuminati, often referred to as the 'Zionist Satanists' by conservative Christians.

In fact, the Catholic Church is alleged to be the largest baby trafficker in human history, making billions each year by selling Catholic newborns to orphanages, foster homes and undisclosed parties.

Apparently, many religion-backed NGOs and organizations have also emerged who traffic children under the garb of adoption. After Angelina Jolie adopted Zahara in 2005 from Ethiopia, apparently the demand for Ethiopian children became fashionable amongst American adoption homes.

Ethiopia has five million orphans needing homes and the US has millions of homes needing babies. However, according to reporters Andrew Geoghegan and Mary Ann Jolie, most of the American adoptive parents discover only after adoption that most of these children are not orphans, as they were previously assured, but have families whom they miss in addition to a litany of health problems.[13] The children are disoriented and in several cases refuse to adjust. Finally, some adoptive parents have also gone to the length of relocating them to their families. However, these adoption agencies force them away from their families again, and the same cycle is repeated.

A case in point is Christian World Adoptions (CWA) in Ethiopia. Lauryn Gallindo, an American citizen, worked as a facilitator for inter-country adoptions from Cambodia to the US. She supplied hundreds of 'orphans' to US families only to later discover that these so-called orphans had families in Cambodia, and were forcefully separated from

---

[13]Foreign correspondent, 'Ethiopia: Fly away children', ABC, 15 September 2009. Available at <https://www.abc.net.au/foreign/ethiopia---fly-away-children/1430136> Accessed on 6 Nov 2019.

them. In 2004, Gallindo pleaded guilty and served an 18-month prison sentence for visa fraud and money laundering. This was after complaints from some American adoptive parents.

Incidently, Angelina Jolie's first adoptive child Maddox, has been adopted through the offices of Gallindo. Fortunately for Jolie, neither Maddox nor Zahara were illegally trafficked children but genuine orphans. A figure very rare.

※

Like its mother organization, the UN, UNICEF too finds its origin in the League of Nations. The UN was founded in 1920 and headquartered in Geneva in Switzerland. It was created after World War I as a forum for sorting out international disputes.[14] When an unprecedented refugee crisis was created after the World War II, UNICEF was formed to help the world's most vulnerable children.[15]

At the time of its formation and up until later, UNICEF largely stayed away from dealing directly with inter-country adoptions, although they did work with international social service providers involved with adoptions. A clear and transparent pro-adoption position was taken by UNICEF in 2004 which was drafted by Nigel Cantwell, a UNICEF consultant.

Illegal practices in child-adoption have been a serious concern for many decades, particularly, those relating to inter-country adoption. A surprising number of incidents of malpractice during such adoptions were seen in the 1980s which confirmed the fear that the legal and human rights framework for inter-country adoption were inadequate. There was an immediate need for creation of policies to safeguard the rights of children which culminated in the 1989 Convention on the

---

[14]UNICEF, 'Learning from experience: 1946–1979', UNICEF, 22 January 2018. Available at <https://www.unicef.org/stories/learning-experience-19461979> Accessed on 7 Nov 2019.
[15]Ibid.

Rights of the Child (CRC) (Art 21) and the 1993 Hague Convention. The conventions were set in place in order to develop procedure that would create a transparent framework.[16]

An open pro-adoption position was taken by UNICEF in 2004, a position drafted by Cantwell. In a paper published by UNICEF in 2010, the organization confirmed its position, 'UNICEF supports inter-country adoption, when pursued in conformity with the standards and principles of the 1993 Hague Convention on Protection of Children and Co-operation in Respect of Inter-country Adoptions—already ratified by more than 80 countries.'[17]

14.

A few months after Jennifer's trip to Ambernath, her brother and his family along with her father visited her in Ashraya in Chembur. 'My brother is a tailor and he is very poor. He never went to school and grew up on the streets. He still calls me Pinky. I used to give him money and I remember giving gifts to his son and a sari for my sister-in-law. I also gave him a cell phone. This set a bad precedent and they kept expecting much more from me. They thought I would spoil them with loads of money. They thought I had money to throw around. They thought I was very rich,' says Jennifer.

'The first time I saw my father, I thought he was a beggar. Skinny, short, shabbily dressed—he was stinking. He was in and out of an alcoholic rehabilitation centre. I did want to give him some money, but I was afraid that he would go out and buy drinks. So I handed the money to my brother instead. I don't know whether he gave it

---

[16]https://docs.google.com/viewerng/viewer?url=https://defenceforchildren.org/wp-content/uploads/2018/02/Sale-of-Children-and-Illegal-Adoption.pdf

[17]UNICEF's position on Inter-country adoption, 22 July 2010. Available at <https://www.unicef.org/media/media_55412.html>

to my father...he resented my father a lot, especially because he was an alcoholic and gave my mother a hard life. There is no photograph of my father in Christopher's house even today, though my father died in 2010...almost eight years ago.'

※

Christopher is not as articulate as Jennifer and has never been to school. He does manage to speak a smattering of Hindi and English, and is fluent in Marathi. He lives in Ambernath in his parents' hut with his wife and young son, who is around ten years old.

According to Christopher, his parents fought a lot mainly because of his father's alcoholism and unemployment. He denies his mother ever worked. Jennifer did meet up with her maternal aunts and grandparents and later found out that both her maternal aunts were HIV positive and later died of it. 'I believe they were into prostitution,' says Jennifer. Christopher completely denies this when I asked him. Christopher is also cagey about whether their mother remarried, but he at some point disclosed to his sister that their mother 'was a whore'. But, he denied it when I asked him.

※

One day, very early in the morning Jennifer got a call from Christopher. 'Daddy died. In Bandra. We will have to collect his body from there. Aunty Costa just called me. She is also coming. Hurry up Jenny. I will see you at the municipal corporation in Bandra. Just find out from someone in Ashraya how to get there.'

Jennifer was still in a daze. She had smoked up till the wee hours of the morning. She had gone to sleep at 3 a.m. Christopher called at 4.30 a.m. She had barely slept for two hours when the news of her father's death came. Christopher from Ambernath, Aunty Costa (her paternal aunt) from Kalyan and Jennifer from Chembur reached the municipality building around 10 a.m.

They waited for the body to arrive in the municipal van. Jennifer thought about the time two months before when her father had come to Chembur asking for money. She blasted him and never saw him after that. And, now he was dead. His body was found on the streets of Bandra, shrivelled and lying in a heap, reeking of alcohol. Her train of thought was broken when the van arrived. A few people rushed to the van including Jennifer and Christopher. Two men came and callously opened the door of the van clanking loudly. There were unclaimed dead bodies in the van, stacked one on top of the other, and the sudden jerk led to three or four bodies falling with a thud on the ground. 'The bodies were stacked badly. Three of them fell and their heads got busted. There was blood and grey matter all over. I had to see this shit. And this shit only happens in India. There is no respect for the dead. It was nightmarish,' Jennifer recounts.

When they collected Bosco's body, he was smelling. 'It was such a foul smell, I didn't want to go anywhere near him. Besides, I had no attachment, so it was okay.'

Meanwhile, Jennifer had to fight with Aunt Costa to shell out some money for Bosco's funeral. 'At least you owe your brother a decent funeral.' Finally, Aunt Costa relented. At the funeral too, Jennifer refused to go near her father's corpse as it still smelt foul. One distant relative came over to Jennifer and said, 'Pinky, you must go and kiss your dad.'

'I don't want to, man. What's your problem? I don't have no feelings for him, man,' Jennifer explained.

'But, he was a nice man,' the girl insisted. 'You must kiss him.'

'In that case dude, why don't you go and kiss him?'

15.

Known as the Mother of Mercy in the East, Kuan Yin has been worshipped by Buddhists for thousands of years. She is the greatest of the bodhisattvas and embodies total compassion for humanity.

The Kuan Yin Charitable Trust in India was based in Colaba, and meant to embody the principles of the goddess Kuan Yin. But, did it?

Kuan Yin was the Indian counterpart of AIAA and the agency responsible for processing all papers for the children being sent to US adoptive homes. A couple of orphanages were run under the trust where abandoned children were sheltered, although in a number of cases, they forcibly snatched children from their parents and sent them to the 'big fat white man's country' for the big bucks.

You can hit your head against a wall trying to find out the history of the Kuan Yin Trust in India. It has been several years since the trust has become defunct but try Googling it—there is no information about its past doings (or, should I say misdoings) on the Internet. It is quite strange. In today's day of information overload, there is nothing about this trust! It is as if it did not even exist.

The workings of the NGO was overseen by Clarice D'Souza, a Keralite Catholic who was one of the most sought-after persons for sending children abroad for adoption from here. According to some she was 'frail and ugly' and according to others, she was 'very stylish'. Some say she was a 'crook, snatching children unlawfully and selling them for huge profits and living a prosperous life off others' miseries' while others say 'she was just doing her job'. Whatever Clarice was, she remains quite an enigma. You can again hit your head against the wall trying to source information on Clarice without any success. Just like you will about her charitable trust!

And worse still, the lady herself remains tight-lipped about her charitable activities. And that sets you wondering 'why'? Why would she not want to talk at all about her career or the organization and its work?

At 90 plus, Clarice lives alone in her spacious apartment in downtown Mumbai. Her children are all abroad, flourishing from the inheritances their mother profited from the Kuan Yin Trust. That is before it became defunct!

And yes, Clarice is extremely articulate. When I called her the first time, she picked up the phone, which she always does. She was courteous and asked me to call back later as she was busy. When I called her a second time she asked me in her husky voice what I wanted. When I asked her I wanted to know about her social work and about the Kuan Yin Trust, she shocked me by saying, 'I don't want to talk about it, my girl. I am past 90 and not keeping too well and I don't want to get into any trouble.' When I asked her what trouble she was referring to, she immediately clamped up and said she did not want to talk about anything. When I prodded her to tell me the technical details like when was the trust founded, and so on, Clarice said, 'It has closed down so why do you want to know anything about it. Sorry to disappoint you my girl, but I have nothing to say.'

According to Pradeep and Sangeeta, there was a lawyer named Jerry Coelho, who worked in tandem with Clarice, but as I was to find out when I called his residence, Coelho passed away some months before I spoke to Clarice. 'Between them, they misused the law and did all the hera pheri and misdeeds,' says Pradeep. 'Coelho was there to bail out the wrongdoings of Clarice and Kuan Yin.'

In an interview given to Arun Dohle some years before he passed away, Coelho admitted that in his legal career spanning nearly four decades, he had processed over two thousand inter-country adoption papers. I decided to call the Coelho residence again in February 2015.

When I called his widow, Mercy, it was his daughter Monisha who took the call and spoke to me at length. An extremely articulate third-generation lawyer (her grandfather was a magistrate of the small causes court), Monisha is now settled abroad (either in the US or Canada). She refused to disclose her current country of residence. When I asked her for Clarice's contact address, she drew a complete blank by asking me: 'Who is she?' When I explained her father's association with the latter, she said he never mentioned her in all these decades of his association with the trust. She asked me, 'Is she alive?' When I replied in the affirmative, she stammered but with surety, 'I'll be honest with you. I do not think, from the name you are telling me, that the person would be involved in trafficking. She could be naive. In those days, rules were very strict. Every matter went through courts and every matter had to go through government agencies. I remember my dad telling me.' Yet, her dad forgot to mention Clarice with whom he had the longest professional association. By defending Clarice, was she defending her father indirectly?

Having been a lawyer in India and working with the human rights legal network of the Collins Group, Monisha denied having heard of CARA or AIAA. But, she did emphasize that once a child has been sent for adoption in another country, like the US, and if the adoption fails, then 'the child goes into US foster care. The highest number of child prostitution cases comes from the US foster care which is notorious for its broken foster care system.'

The only source of information available on Clarice and her agency was from the affidavit that she produced under oath in court on 20 June 1989. It says: 'I, Mrs Clarice D'Souza is a trustee of the Kuan Yin Charitable Trust located at 91 Advent, 12A General Bhonsle Marg, Mumbai 400 021.'

On surfing the net I came across a very interesting post by Vanessa from Canada during an appeal from children affected by inter-country adoption worldwide. Here is what Vanessa had to say about Clarice and the Kuan Yin Charitable Trust:

I am an adoptee born in India and my adoption was also handled by Clarice D'Souza of the now defunct Kuan Yin Charitable Trust. I was stolen from my family and adopted to a family who had been found unfit to adopt children, yet Clarice let them adopt me. I faced years of sexual and physical abuse at the hands of my adoptive parents until I was taken into foster care where I faced more abuse. I had been stolen from my family and records were falsified as well. I am still searching for my family and I desperately hope to find them one day. I want to see this woman Clarice brought to justice for what she has done to Indian children.

And that in a nutshell says it all about Clarice and her activities with regard to the Kuan Yin Charitable Trust. Even if they did manage to wipe out their past activities by wiping out all the information from the net, there will be enough Vanessas and Jennifers in the world who are living testimony to their misdeeds.

16.

Sometime in 1979, a young Bosco Francis happened to come over from Ulhasnagar in Thane to visit his cousins in Ambernath.

Like all Mumbai suburbs Ambarnath is divided into eastern and western zones by the railway line. The western part is an industrial zone dotted with many small chemical factories and the famous ordnance factory. The eastern part used to be earlier dotted with bungalows and was known as pensioners' paradise, but today it is buzzing with a working population. With its many factories, Ambernath appears to be a dustier and poorer area of Thane today.

Ambernath is spread over an area of 38 sq. km with a dense population of 20,000/sq. km. In addition to the Ayappa Temple, there is also a Shiva Temple, as well as a number of churches such as the Fatima Catholic Church and the Sacred Heart Malabar Catholic Church. It is but obvious that despite being in the state of Maharashtra with Marathi as the official language, it is the Malabar Catholics who dominate the population here after having relocated from their native state of Kerala. While criminals like Walekar and Karanjule have given Ambernath a bad name, former Olympian hockey player Merwyn Fernandes and international footballer Evaristo Cardozo have also made this little hamlet proud.

A member of one such Malabar Catholic family, Bosco Francis was visiting was his first cousin Wilma Francis in Ambernath. Wilma was his paternal uncle's daughter, who lived with her parents and two sisters in what was considered a more affluent part of eastern Ambernath, though they were not rich by any means. Only they happened to live in a 'flat' as apartments were known as in these parts. Wilma was very pretty and Bosco was immediately smitten by his extremely pretty and petite cousin, whose dark curls framed her dimpled countenance and warm smile. Wilma also found the skinny and awkward-looking Bosco attractive and liked his shyness. But despite seeking permission, both sets of parents were opposed to Bosco and Wilma's marriage. Wilma was in a hurry to settle down away from the comforts of her home. And, even a poor plumber like Bosco without a stable job and despite parental opposition, would do for her as long as she was away from her folks.

One does wonder about the reason for Wilma's hurry to marry and leave home, as she was very young, barely out of her teens, at the time. There were many theories to this, and the neighbourhood tongues wagged about the dubious nature of activities Wilma and her sisters were involved in.

After marriage—or perhaps there was no marriage, as their marriage was never solemnized either in a court or in a church—the young couple went and settled in a little rented room in Ulhasnagar, about

30 km from her parental home.

Almost 60 km outside Mumbai, Ulhasnagar also known as Sindhunagar has the largest population of Hindu Sindhis outside Sindh. The members of this community were all engaged in small businesses. The largest manufacturers of denim, fake perfumes and other inexpensive electronic goods outside China thrive here. The joke among Indians and their craving for 'foreign-made' goods is that when anything says, 'Made in USA' it would normally stand for 'Made in Ulhasnagar Sindhi Association'.

In 1977, a son Christopher was born to Wilma and Bosco. Soon after, things started to deteriorate between the couple. Bosco was mostly out of work and drinking very often. There was verbal and physical abuse, and Wilma decided to move back to Ambernath with her young son though their official address still remained Ulhasnagar 4. Bosco followed. First she moved in with her mother and sisters, then they rented a small room and very soon Bosco managed to save enough to buy a small house, basically a small one-room plus kitchen space with just enough legroom space for a bath. It was barely 150 sq. feet in all. This was near the Shiva temple, in the poor hutment areas of the town. The house number was 4444 and remains the same till date.

On a rainy day on 29 September 1981, Wilma gave birth to a baby girl.

'Mummy look here...baby's cheeks are so pinky pink,' four-year-old Christopher chuckled excitedly looking into the completely wrinkled little pink bundle which lay by his mother's side.

Wilma smiled.

'Hey boy,' his grandmother yelled from the kitchen as she hurriedly came to the bedroom, 'For Christ's sake don't say such unlucky things.'

'Why unlucky?' Christopher asked innocently.

'Because pink newborns grow up to be dark. You want a fair sister na?'

'No, I don't want a fair or dark sister. I like this pinky sister. Mummy we will call her Pinky. Okay?'

'Okay.' Wilma smiled.

※

Around 2013, Jennifer and her friend went to the Bombay Municipal Corporation (BMC) office and searched for a birth certificate in vain. But there was none, so in all probability she was born at home. The only proof is her baptismal certificate.

Pinky was christened at Fatima's Church as Jennifer Pinky Francis on 9 January 1983. Her address was given as Ulhasnagar 4 because the Francises had not moved into House No.4444 yet. Bosco put down his profession as 'service' in the baptismal certificate, though he continued as an unemployed plumber mostly. Both her godparents, Totto Middleton and Gunnie Charles were from Ambernath and the minister who baptized Pinky was Rev. Father U. Fernandes.

※

Christopher or Jony as he is fondly referred to remembers playing with little Pinky. But the memories are hazy. All he remembers were days of extreme poverty and deprivation where the family went without food for days. Bosco was now spending more time in Bombay working as a plumber. Though Christopher insists their mother stayed at home looking after them, Pinky clearly remembers her mother working as a domestic help in various houses. Fearing to leave a young female child at home and attracting unwanted attention from undesirable people, Wilma used to take little Pinky along with her to the homes where she worked as a housemaid.

The common childhood memory of the siblings apart from poverty is the fact that they have vivid recollections of their parents quarrelling, which would turn into ugly fights. Whenever Bosco returned from his work trips from Bombay, he would first abuse Wilma verbally and physically. According to Christopher, his mother seldom retaliated and as a result she harboured a life-long anger against his father. Jennifer was too small to realize the reason for the fights but she does remember her father as an abusive alcoholic.

※

One recurrent childhood dream Jennifer had for a very long time involved her lying on a white bedsheet in their little room and a young boy, not much older than her, trying to violate her and fondle her private parts. Most often the face would be of her brother, Christopher. It was something she was not able to tell anyone until recently when she confided in me. She was terribly ashamed of it, and also unsure of its authenticity.

'I kept having recurring dreams of being raped by my brother,' Jennifer almost mumbles in hurt and shame. 'I started bed-wetting since then and couldn't stop till the time I got married. Almost till nineteen years of age,' she reveals.

Having gone over this incident with Jennifer, it did occur to us both that perhaps she did as a child confess to her mother about her nightmares of Christopher violating her. Her mother must have been too aghast or too ashamed. Whatever the reason, she must have been ashamed at her own son's misdoings and in order to keep the family skeletons hidden, she may have started to take Pinky with her to her places of work. She was scared of leaving Pinky alone, and the excuse that the area was not safe and was full of drug dealers selling weed and brown sugar came in handy.

Around this time Wilma was working for a Mr Brown. Though Christopher denies his mother working, it is true from Pinky's childhood memories that her mother managed the household expenses during her father's absence. Things between parents deteriorated to the point that Wilma left the house one day with Pinky and moved in with Mr Brown. But Wilma was told by Mr Brown to put the child in an orphanage or boarding school run by missionaries. 'I really have no idea what was the real situation or why my parents fought. Or what kind of work my mother really did?'

After a pregnant pause, almost mumbling with moist eyes, Jennifer reveals, 'I dunno how true it is but I have been told that my mother was a whore.'

17.

The aroma of the chicken stew being slow-cooked in coconut milk drifted across from the kitchen as little Pinky was playing with a one-armed plastic doll in the garden outside the kitchen. The doll was a castaway from Gerry Brown's daughter Lydia. Smelling the food Pinky started bawling loudly. 'What's it now?' Wilma yelled from the kitchen. '*Kaiko rotey* Pinky?' (Why are you crying, Pinky?)

'*Bhoonkh lagley* (I am hungry.) *Zevan deya* (I want food),' the five-year-old bawled in fluent Marathi.

'Okay. Okay baba. Here. Come in and eat.'

Pinky happily skipped towards the kitchen.

'Come here *chinamma*,' Wilma called Pinky and gestured her to sit on the floor near the kitchen door. She handed her a shiny steel plate with a *chappati* and a little sugar on the side. 'Eat Pinky, eat.' But, to her surprise, Pinky started bawling again.

'*Ata kaye?*' (Now what?) Wilma asked surprised.

'I want chicken curry, Mummy. I know you are making chicken *ishtew*. I want *ishtew*.'

'Shh. Shh. Chup. I will lose my job if I give you *ishtew*. That is for the guests in the evening. Gerry Uncle is having some friends over. Some Clarice Madam is coming. She is very big person and rich lady running many schools. She is coming and wants to have *appam* with *ishtew*.' Saying this Wilma quietly slipped in a ladleful of gravy with a sliver of chicken on to Pinky's plate. 'Now stop crying and eat quickly before anyone catches us.' Pinky hungrily walloped the food.

※

Bosco was in Bombay working as a plumber in the new upcoming buildings, and away for months together. Whenever he came he was either drinking and abusing Wilma or just gave her some money to run the house. The latter happened infrequently. Wilma realized it was useless depending on her husband's largesse which was as moody as him.

She decided to work as a housemaid in several houses. The most recent one was at the house of a Gerry Brown or Mr Brown as he was known in the neighbourhood. Mr Brown kept the Church accounts and that is where Wilma met him. He was looking for a housekeeper and Father Fernandes knowing of Wilma's financial hardship introduced her to him.

Gerry Brown was very clever with numbers and he was what they called a chartered accountant. Not only did he look after the accounts of the Fatima Church, he also worked as part-time accountant for several schools and orphanages like St Anthony's Home and St Joseph's Home, among others. Most of these homes were under the aegis of the Kuan Yin Charitable Trust which was overseen by Clarice.

Gerry's wife, Mary, was a Malabar Catholic like him from Kerala. She had inherited large properties in her native Ernakulam, and being the only child in a matriarchal society, she was stationed there overseeing the large banana plantations. Their daughter about ten years old also stayed with Mary. In fact, no one in Ambernath knew Mr Brown was married or had a wife as nobody had seen Mrs Mary Brown. The only proof of her in the little bungalow Gerry Brown stayed in near the Fatima Church compound was a family photograph of the Browns on the upright piano that was hardly ever played. But Wilma always dusted it clean so that the wood gleamed even though the keys were dusty.

※

The Francis family had settled into a routine in Bosco's absence. Wilma woke up by six in the morning and cleaned the little room that was her home. She got the children ready and by seven they were out of the house. Christopher, nearly ten by this time, was dropped off at the market where he helped a vegetable dealer doing odd jobs and carting sacks of vegetables on his little shoulders. As he recollects now, 'Mainey bahut bojh uthaiya.' (I have carried heavy burdens.)

Christopher worked all day till nearly eight in the evening. In return he was rewarded with tea and bread in the mornings and evenings and a plate of rice, dal and vegetables for lunch. This was enough to sustain him. He returned home at night, and the only entertainment for the siblings was to watch their mother cook dinner. By means of a salary, he received a hundred and fifty rupees at the end of the month which went into the family coffers.

After dropping Christopher to his workplace, Wilma would take Pinky to the houses where she worked. Now that she had given up all her other work in order to work for Gerry Brown, it was not so bad. She made breakfast and packed his lunch before he left for work. Since Mr Brown was away at work during the day, Wilma and Pinky had the house to themselves. Pinky played with his daughter's broken toys while Wilma cleaned and cooked. They also had their meals at Mr Brown's. Once work was done, Wilma and Pinky watched some black-and-white films on the little box in the living room till Gerry Brown came home at six.

Then Wilma got busy fussing over him and serving him snacks and other goodies she cooked during the day. Pinky noticed her mother was coy in his presence. She felt a little resentment but continued to keep herself entertained. It really did not matter. She was a happy child.

By nine o'clock, after serving Mr Brown dinner, especially the *chappatis* which he insisted being served hot while eating, and after clearing up the kitchen, Wilma returned to her house to cook the meal for her family. Lately, Mr Brown insisted she cook and take food from his house which not only made it easier, but the food was a lot tastier than the hurriedly cooked dinner the children were served.

※

This evening Wilma's culinary skills were at their best. She had made traditional *medu vadas* and served with coconut chutney and fried *rawas* or kingfish while Mr Brown and his guests, including Clarice and another gentleman, enjoyed it with their drinks. The evening started early as the guests had a long drive back to Bombay.

Clarice 'Madam' was an extremely stylish lady in a bob cut hairstyle, wearing fine jewels and a pretty floral dress. She coordinated it with a stylish cream-coloured purse and matching ballerina shoes. Her pearl drops and strands completed the ensemble. Her long varnished nails in crimson, held a cigarette in one hand and a glass of Merlot in the other as she spoke and puffed smoky rings simultaneously.

'My my, what a chirpy little girl,' Clarice called to Jennifer who kept flittering about in her Sunday best. That was the only dress she had which she wore to Church. Today was special as Mr Brown was having 'special guests' so Wilma saw to it that Pinky was well-dressed.

'What is your name, my child?' Clarice asked.

'Pinky.'

'Actually her name is Jennifer, Madam. We call her Pinky at home,' Wilma added.

'Ah. I see. And which class are you in my dear?' Clarice continued while Jennifer looked blank.

'Clarice, the child doesn't go to school yet. They cannot afford schooling for her,' Gerry explained.

'Oh. I see,' Clarice said. 'Such a shame. In that case Gerry why don't you bring her to my school. I will see what I can do for her. A bright girl like her should not be wasted scurrying around doing nothing,' smiled Clarice.

'Yes, I will,' Gerry replied.

'Madam, thank you so much,' Wilma smiled at Clarice with folded hands. 'I want her to study. Pinky is very smart. Smarter than her brother. I will be very grateful to you Madam if you will teach my Pinky,' Wilma blabbered.

'Of course, I will, my girl,' Clarice smiled.

The evening ended with Wilma's lip-smacking chicken *ishtew* and *appam*. And a hope for a promising future for Pinky.

※

'Why do you have to go back to an empty house every day?' Gerry asked Wilma after their frantic love-making in his bedroom one evening. Pinky was sitting in the living room glued to the television.

'Where empty Saar? My children are with me *na*...'

'Yes. Yes. I know. But you can stay here. There is an extra room. You and Jenny can both stay here,' Gerry said. 'That way you can save the hundred rupees rent.'

'And what about my son? Jony?' Wilma asked.

'Ah. Yes. I completely forgot about Jony,' Gerry crinkled his brows. He did not want the growing boy living with him. The place would get too cramped. 'Why don't you let him live with your mom? His aunts can look after him...'

'No. I don't think that is possible,' Wilma broke in.

'At least you can try?' Gerry persuaded. 'Besides, your mother's house is closer to the main market and it will be quicker for Jony to reach home every evening. Plus, he can come and visit us on Sundays and we can all go to Church together.'

'Hmmm...let me see,' Wilma pondered.

'Besides, my darling,' Gerry pulled Wilma towards him pushing her curls behind while kissing her upturned nose, 'I want you here with me all the time.'

'Saar,' Wilma smiled coyly, 'I will then not be free to do other work...'

'Shh...quiet my darling. I don't want you to work anywhere else.' Gerry Brown figured what Wilma Francis was getting at. The brass tacks. 'I will give you a hundred per cent raise. You will get eight hundred rupees every month now. And, you will live like my queen.'

Wilma could not believe her ears. From four hundred rupees, a straight hike to eight hundred rupees! Did she hear right? 'You are sure, Saar?'

'Yes Wilma. Sure.'

'*Nakki* Saar?'

'*Nakki*. It's a deal then?' Gerry asked. Wilma Francis nodded.

And that is how Pinky and her mother came to stay at Mr Brown's bungalow while Jony stayed with his grandparents and aunts. Bosco was furious when he found out and walked the streets drunk, yelling in the middle of the night in front of Gerry Brown's bungalow, 'My wife is Brown's concubine.'

It was many years later, perhaps after hearing his father's drunken accusations or simply feeling abandoned because of his mother's behaviour, Christopher would tell his sister that maybe their mother was a 'whore'.

18.

Days slipped into months with Wilma and Pinky staying with Mr Brown and Jony at his grandparents. Pinky romped around the bungalow through the day while her mother did the household chores. Mother and daughter spent quality time together. In the evenings however when Mr Brown returned, her mother's attention was taken over by him. Pinky resented this. She would find ways to distract her mother while she was busy pampering her paramour.

Many a time, Pinky would get up with a start in the middle of the night to find her mother gone. She would run towards Gerry Uncle's room and hear their voices. Sometimes, she would knock loudly and wake them or disturb their conversations. Gerry was beginning to find Pinky a nuisance.

One day Gerry casually asked Clarice about Pinky's education. 'Ah Gerry, yes. You mean that little brat! She must be quite a handful, right?' the woman winked at Gerry. 'Bring her tomorrow to St Joseph's and let me arrange a place for her there.' Gerry was only too happy and agreed.

※

Though Wilma had agreed about Jennifer's education, she was not keen to put her in a boarding school. And worse still, little Pinky refused to be parted from her mother. But Gerry convinced Wilma. 'It is for Pinky's good. For her future, my darling.' Wilma finally agreed.

The next day the trio headed to St Joseph's Nursery & Home in Byculla. It was an NPO, functioning under the aegis of the Kuan Yin Charitable Trust for young abandoned children. Jennifer was scared and sad and peed a lot in bed. Wilma visited her a couple of times and assured her daughter that she would grow up to be a 'smart girl' if she stayed here and studied hard. Little Pinky had no choice; she missed home and her brother Jony.

Three months later, Clarice removed her from St Joseph's Home and put her in St Anthony's Home & School in the same area.

This home had high schools for boys and girls in separate buildings as well as a shelter for abandoned and orphaned children. All housed together in a common compound. Since Pinky had not been to school and she was nearing seven, she was put in the lowest grade. She stayed in the shelter home and an older girl Karen, who worked in the shelter was assigned to take care of her.

Jennifer's memories of the time spent in St Anthony's are hazy. 'I was very sad and very scared to leave my home. I was bed-wetting and so was made to sleep on the floor. I still do till date. All I remember was sleeping on the floor. There were other kids and I had a doll that I always carried. Beyond that I remember very little.'

❦

Meanwhile when Bosco returned from his stints, he was furious to know that his daughter was put in a shelter home without his permission. The drunk Bosco accused his wife of whoring around and selling his daughter. He threatened to call the police and accused Gerry Brown of pimping.

'Go. Go. I don't want to talk to a drunkard. You are not man enough to look after your family,' Wilma retaliated. Christopher remembers many such drunken brawls and fights and accusations thrown against each other by his parents. 'Daddy was very fond of Pinky. He was heartbroken when he learnt she was sent to the home. He wanted to see her but was not allowed to. He started to drink even more,' recollects Christopher.

Not only was Bosco denied permission to meet his daughter, Wilma too was discouraged by Clarice from visiting Pinky. 'Gerry please tell her that every time she visits Jennifer, the poor child goes into depression and her studies are affected. Let the child settle in and then I will call Wilma over. Till then my boy, handle her,' Clarice cooed.

❦

'Hi George,' the scarlet lips huskily cooed into the black mouthpiece, 'This is Clarice here. From Kuan Yin Trust, Bombay.'
'Hey! Hi Clarice. Good to hear from you. What a surprise!' George Hancox replied from Laurenceville in Gwinnett County, Georgia.
  'George I will need you to come down immediately. I have exactly what you are looking for,' Clarice continued. 'Meanwhile, I will send you a photograph. She is beautiful. All of seven...seven-and-a-half. Just came into our home. Poor kid has been totally abandoned due to poverty.'

'Oh Clarice. How can I thank you enough. You send me her picture and I will come right away,' Hancox said.

※

'Gerry, I need to have a little confidential talk with you. That's why I needed to meet you,' Clarice sat in her private office of the trust in Colaba.

'I hope the accounts are in order?' Gerry looked worried.

'Oh no. They are fine. Coffee?' Gerry Brown nodded a no.

'Well, it's like this, Gerry. A lovely rich couple from the US would love to adopt a six- or seven-year-old Indian girl. They already have an eighteen-year-old boy. The mother cannot have any more children so they need a little girl to complete the family,' Clarice explained. Gerry almost figured what the old woman was getting at when Clarice said, 'To put it bluntly, I cannot think of anyone but Jennifer.'

'Oh. No. No, no, no, Clarice. That is impossible. Wilma will never agree. You will have to find another girl for this couple. Getting her to agree to put the girl in the boarding was difficult enough and now giving her up for adoption…how did you even think of it Clarice!'

'Gerry, my boy,' Clarice said calmly as she puffed at her cigarette, 'Who says we are giving Jennifer away for adoption. Tsk, tsk, tsk… never. We are only sending her there to study so that when she returns at eighteen, she will have a bright future here,' Clarice smiled.

Gerry quite familiar with Clarice's wheeling and dealings asked, 'And, will Jennifer ever return?'

'Ah. That remains to be seen. We will deal with that when we cross the bridge,' Clarice said pulling out a stamped legal paper. 'Now all you have to do is get Wilma to sign on this saying she is unable to take care of her child and therefore giving her up for adoption.'

'Clarice…'

'And Gerry there is going to be a little reward for us in this, you understand?' Clarice continued unfazed.

'But Clarice…'

'Some coffee now, Gerry?'
'But Clarice you...'
'Get me the paper tomorrow, my boy—signed.'

Jennifer's 38-year-old brother Christopher, who was a little over ten at the time, remembers the huge fight that broke out between his parents when Bosco found out that Jennifer was to be sent to the US.

'Arrey! Are you mad, Wilma? How can you let your daughter go to Amrica. They will take her away forever. We will never see her ever.' Bosco was hysterical.

'Oh keep quiet. She is only going for studies...'

'Arrey! They will use her for prostitution. They will take away her organs and sell them...' Bosco led out a wail.

Recollecting those incidents, Christopher says, 'I remember my sister was in a boarding school in Bombay and when my mother went to meet her a second time, she was told that Jennifer had been sent to Amrica for studies. She was shocked and had a big fight with the head of the school, but it was useless as no one listened to her and told her that she had given a thumb impression on a paper to send her to Amrica.'

'My mother kept telling my father and me that she had only sent Pinky for education in Bombay and not Amrica. She did not know how to fight back and kept waiting for her daughter to return after eighteen. My mother suffered extreme sorrow, pain and mental torture for Pinky and finally died in April 2006 without ever seeing her.'

'I was also a child at the time my mother kept Pinky in school, so I was not able to do anything for my sister.'

As Clarice stepped into her room in the Kuan Yin Trust office in Colaba, she heard the phone ring. The tone indicated it was a long-distance call, which was nothing surprising as the trust mainly dealt with inter-country adoptions.

'Yes. Clarice D'Souza here,' she said into the mouthpiece as she lifted the receiver. There was a little pause and then the voice on the other end said, 'Hi there, Clarice. This is George Hancox here. From Laurenceville, Georgia.'

'Ah yes. Tell me George, when are you coming?'

'Ah, that's why I called. You see, it will be impossible for me to come now as I have no leaves left at work. Both Melissa and I have seen Jennifer's photograph and we both like her. Why don't you process the papers from your end while we do what needs to be done from our end through AAIA, and then I will send you the cheque? You can send Jennifer with an airline escort and we will collect her from the airport here,' George explained.

'Oh. Ok,' Clarice said. Internally, she was delighted that she would not have to deal with the Hancoxes directly. There were too many explanations to give and too many acts to put up. 'I will take care of all that. You need not worry. But are you sure you do not want to see your daughter before you adopt her?'

'It's ok Clarice. We liked what we saw in the photograph. The rest we trust you. We leave it to you.'

'Alright, my love. I will do as you say. Also don't forget to send the cheque as soon as possible. Bye bye.'

'I will. Bye.'

19.

On 20 June 1989, Clarice D'Souza as a Trustee of the Kuan Yin Charitable Trust filed an affidavit of Jennifer's birth and abandonment certificate in the Bombay High Court, appointing herself as the legal guardian of the minor girl as she was 'an absolutely abandoned destitute'. In the same affidavit she also 'irrevocably consent[ed] to the immigration and adoption of Jennifer to the USA' since Jennifer was an 'abandoned destitute'.

※

Apart from the abandonment certificate, Clarice also produced in court Jennifer's baptismal certificate, which she claimed Wilma gave her before she 'relinquished Jennifer'.

In a memo signed by Clarice on 19 July 1990, Jennifer's mother Wilma gave away Jennifer voluntarily as she was ill. Clarice said she first met Wilma in 1988 when she came with Jennifer to the trust office to relinquish her daughter voluntarily as she was ill and jobless. She was living in the house of a Mr Brown who could not keep them any longer. Also, even if she could manage to leave Jennifer in a rented accommodation go to work, she feared the child would be sexually abused as the area was infested with alcoholics and drug addicts. She had kept her in St Joseph's Home but they told her to leave after three months. Since she was ill and impoverished, she wanted to give the child up for adoption as she had no other choice.

According to Clarice, Jennifer appeared happy and friendly and not perturbed, apparently because her mother must have prepared her for a new family. Clarice then took her to St Anthony's Home in a taxi and Jennifer told Clarice that she loved 'taxi rides as much as she loved her mother and chocolates'.

In reality, Jennifer kept bed-wetting at St Anthony's because she was insecure about losing her parents and going into a new home. She kept waiting for her mother to visit her and when her mother did not, she felt very helpless and abandoned. She confided in one of the social workers, Karen, 'I've got a Mummy but she doesn't want me.'

Clarice went on to state that while the case was in court, Karen was sent to meet Jennifer's mother who had just married and was in hospital for a re-anastomose surgery as she wanted to have another child with her new husband. According to Clarice's version, Wilma's new husband did not want Jennifer. The case was passed and Wilma thanked Clarice for finding a new home for Jennifer. Clarice went on to state that even though Jennifer was excited about travelling to 'Amrica' she was nevertheless sad at leaving the home.

Clarice concludes in the memo:

> In conclusion I would like to say this. It requires courage and love to relinquish a child at seven years of age. Jennifer's mother had both these qualities as she wished the best for her child. She saw no hope for the child's future if she continued to live with her. She would not have had the opportunity for marriage as Indian society still frowns on unwed motherhood. She also displayed the fine quality of gratitude with her telephone call after the case was passed. I am writing all this for the future when Jennifer's emotions about her relinquishment may surface. I want to reiterate that her mother loved her.

The questions that arise from Clarice D'Souza's memo are as follows:

First, regarding Wilma, Clarice states: 'She would not have the opportunity for marriage as Indian society still frowns on unwed motherhood.' In what way was Wilma an unwed mother. She was already a married woman with two children as is evident from Jennifer's baptismal certificate. And, why is there is no mention of her son Christopher?

Second, if 'Jennifer seemed happy and unperturbed' about going to live with a new family, then why did she continue bed-wetting or keep waiting for her mother to visit her?

Even after all these years, Jennifer insists, 'My mother put me into an orphanage as she was illiterate and was misled into believing it was a charitable school where I would get an education and food and shelter. Though Mrs Clarice D'Souza told me that my mother had abandoned me, I find it still hard to believe. I loved my mother very much and I did not think she would give me away.'

20.

'Jennifer, my girl,' Sister Claire called out to Jennifer. 'Come here. Karen is waiting to take you to Uncle Jo's. Come on. Hurry up. You will be late for your classes.'

'Coming, coming,' Jennifer ran towards the gate where Karen was waiting for her. 'Sister, Sandra also come. She and me also. Both learn English. Jo Uncle teach. With me too,' Jennifer said pointing out to her playmate Sandra, whom she just abandoned to head to her English classes. The classes were held at Joseph Sequera's house, just outside St Anthony's Home. Everyone called him Uncle Jo and he gave special English classes to children from the home, especially those who had to learn the language in a quick span. Children like Jennifer.

St Anthony's Home in Byculla where Jennifer was staying housed a church on the ground floor and the destitute children's hostel above it. Then across the lawns from the hostel was the school. Jennifer remembered her best friend in St Anthony's, Sandra, as a short and dark girl. They did everything together. 'We played, studied and even slept on the floor together,' recalls Jennifer. 'Evenings were the best time as we played together on the grounds after school. Sometimes we even played on the terrace above the hostel.'

One day Sister Claire, who was Jennifer's favourite nun in the home, told her that she would soon go to a new home with a new 'mummy' and 'daddy'. Little Pinky felt nothing—neither joy nor sorrow. Not even curiosity. All she knew was that she had to take special English classes as her new 'parents' spoke only English.

Sister Claire told Jennifer, 'You will be going to your new home,' but did not tell her where. It was then that Jennifer broke down. She had come to like the home. She did not want to leave Sandra or Karen or Sister Claire and go away. Though she was excited to be dressed in a new frock, she kept crying as she bade goodbye to her friends in the home.

She and a pair of twin girls, 'very small babies and very cute' along with two ladies were sent away. 'I remember being put in a large wicker picnic basket. I was very thin and small for my age so I fitted into one basket and the twins were put in another. I stayed curled up in the basket and the lid was closed. I felt suffocated. It was an uncomfortable ride.'

The children were taken to a hotel room with their two lady escorts and another lady came and some paper work was conducted. Throughout the journey the twins cried; Jennifer did the same, intermittently. The next day, two other ladies came and put the children in baskets again and took them to the airport. At the airport they were handed over to two women who took charge of the children. One lady took the twins away while the other took Jennifer to an airplane. 'I don't remember her name but she was fat. I don't even remember the plane journey. I just remember crying and then falling asleep.'

In April 1989, Clarice D'Souza was granted guardianship of Jennifer Pinky Francis by the Bombay High Court.

Soon after she facilitated Jennifer's adoption with George and Melissa Hancox of Lawrenceville, Georgia, US. The strange part was that the Hancoxes never visited Jennifer or even came to India. What is even stranger was the fact that Clarice dealt only with George Hancox. During the entire procedure of adopting Jennifer, Melissa stayed away from the picture. It was George who decided on the adoption with Clarice. Melissa was merely a 'signatory'.

'Mr and Mrs Hancox never visited me when I was in India,' says Jennifer. 'Though they did send medicines for me as I was very weak and mangy. The first time I met them was when I arrived in Georgia as an eight year old.'

21.

On a cold day on 3 February 1990, Jennifer stepped on to American soil in Seattle, Washington. Her Indian passport contained no last names of her parents. Clarice D'Souza was named as an emergency contact.

At the airport Jennifer was handed over to a white American lady, who was a social worker. At this point and having had so many changes of guardianships in a span of just few days, little Jennifer started bawling as she touched American soil.

'Come, my child. Your long journey will soon be over. Just a little bit more travelling left and then you will meet your new mama and dada and they will love you and buy you lots of toys,' the lady said as they got into a cab. The cab stopped in front of a hotel and little Jennifer's carry case was off-loaded and the lady held her hands and took her to a restaurant in the hotel. It was sometime early in the evening.

Seated at a corner table, at the farthest end of the near empty restaurant, was a white American couple. They stood up as Jennifer walked towards them and the woman came towards Jennifer. She reached out for Jennifer's little hand and knelt down as she held it, 'Oh my God. You are so pretty. How I have been waiting for you my dear,' she said.

'Jennifer. This is your new mummy,' the social worker introduced her to the very thin, pale and greying Melissa Hancox. 'And this, Jennifer,' the lady continued, 'Is your new daddy.'

'Hi. How's my girl,' George Hancox said. 'Welcome, welcome.' Jennifer looked at the heavy-set, balding, pink-faced, big-bellied man, beaming like a Santa Claus. Perplexed, Jennifer started bawling again.

'Oh my poor baby. Shh. Shh. Don't cry. Mama and Dada are here. All will be okay. Everything will be fine,' Melissa comforted her.

'I remember they were nice, but I was just too exhausted. And maybe too overwhelmed.'

They stayed the night at the Seattle hotel of which Jennifer remembers nothing at all. She remembers taking a flight to Atlanta the next day.

'The best part of Atlanta was my new parents taking me to a mall. It was huge. All of eleven storeys. I had seen nothing like that before. They bought me a lot of stuff...clothes, toys, and sweets and chocolates. I was very happy. I forgot all my sadness,' is all Jennifer recollects of her first day in America.

※

Lawrenceville is a suburb of Georgia with a population of approximately 30,000. The city was named after naval commander James Lawrence, whose famous dying statement during the War of 1812, was 'Don't give up the ship'. Lawrenceville's most historical building is the Gwinnett Historical Courthouse in downtown, and few know that one of its most famous resident was Oliver Hardy, one half of the world famous comic duo Lauren & Hardy, who lived there as a child in around 1900.

※

The eight-year-old Jennifer arrived in Lawrenceville to live with George and Melissa at 2546 Cruze Road. George, a big burley school bus mechanic by profession and a hunter by passion and his wife, Melissa, a teacher and social worker, were a typical Lawrenceville couple. They lived in a pretty suburban house while their only child, eighteen-year-old Brent was away in college.

Little Jennifer was very excited when she saw her new parents' home. 'It was a very pretty white-coloured house on the main road.' Indeed, 2546 was a typical suburban American house. There was a driveway into the house past a mailbox, and Jennifer entered her new home through the side entrance by the garage into the kitchen and the dining area.

'Just outside the kitchen was the living area followed by George and Melissa's bedroom on the right-hand side. There was a fireplace and above that was a stuffed deer head. Dad was a hunter and he hunted a lot. Opposite side of the fireplace was the television and facing it on one side was Dad's rocking chair. Next to that was Mom's chair where she sat and sewed a lot. We would call it the sewing chair. She used to knit a lot too,' Jennifer's memory of the house is vivid after all these years.

Above the staircase on the right-hand side was Jennifer's bedroom all done up in pink, with pretty curtains and a canopy bed. There was also a Barbie house that Jennifer played with a lot and a cassette player with a cassette playing the American national anthem. The bathroom was outside in the corridor and common for Brent and Jennifer. Brent's room was across Jennifer's, but he was never home being mostly away in college. But what made Jennifer really happy was the little portable black and white television which was Brent's and which she would take along with her all over the house. 'My favourite shows were Vicky the Robot and Life Goes On,' she says.

'I was very happy to have a room and toys to myself. I was very happy with the Hancoxes. And I also stopped bed-wetting during the period I was there,' Jennifer reveals.

'Since Dad used to be a bus mechanic and fix old school buses, we had an old one in the yard where I used to go and play in there. We also had a dog, I remember. And there was a Korean family who lived next door and I used to play with their daughter. She was my friend, but I can't remember her name.'

Soon, Jennifer was put in day care as both George and Melissa went out to work. Melissa worked as a sign-language teacher. George would drop her off to day care and Melissa would pick her up on way home. 'I remember I used to pull Mom's hair and trouble her and just be plain rude to her, though she used to be very patient with me,' recollects Jennifer. 'I remember the time she patiently taught me to tie laces. Even today whenever I tie a lace, I think of her.'

'Brent was kinda cool, though he spoke very little. I remember Mom took me to Pennsylvania to meet up with my cousins, but there really weren't anyone my age. I feel bad now that I was unduly mean to her though she tried her best to make me feel at home.'

Perhaps, Melissa found it difficult to deal with the dysfunctional little girl and soon George took over. Or, maybe she never wanted to adopt a child and was coaxed into it by George. Maybe it was just George's idea to adopt a girl. Whatever the reasons, it was George who bathed and clothed Jennifer and took her out for little picnics alone. An AIAA employee, Myrna McNitt, who was the social worker entrusted to supervise Jennifer, claimed Jennifer told her that George took her out alone for picnics and 'played bed games' thereby insinuating 'sexual abuse'. In fact, it was Myrna's report that made the supervising agency remove Jennifer from the Hancox home, barely a year after she was 'happy there'.

In her report dated 7 October 1993 to Tom Black, the Protective Services Supervisor in Calhoun County in Battle Creek Michigan, McNitt who was entrusted to supervise Jennifer during her broken placement from the Hancoxes to the Edgells for a year between 1991 and 1992, wrote:

> Jennifer came from India as a declared orphan...Jennifer's early life was spent in extreme poverty...Early in 1993, a relative informed me anonymously to suspect George Hancox of sexually abusing Jennifer...he took her out for picnics alone and played 'bed games' according to Jennifer...

It has been nearly two-and-a-half decades and for the first time Jennifer reacts to McNitt's report about George Hancox sexually abusing her.

'This is pure bullshit man. I never said he abused me sexually. He used to give me a bath and take me out to picnics, like one big water park, but he never did anything out of turn. Know what I mean? He never fondled my body parts or fingered me in the wrong places.'

'On the other hand, I clearly remember being sexually abused at the Edgells. According to the reports, I was sexually violated before reaching the Edgells. If so, I don't remember when or how, apart from those recurring images of my brother, Christopher. But certainly not George Hancox. If I can remember incidents at 4–5 years of age, I certainly would have remembered what happened to me at 8–9 years.'

'I have a feeling the Edgells must have manipulated the report to save their asses. Maybe I was brainwashed into blaming George then. I can't remember. Besides, the muthafukka Blaine Edgell was quite politically well-connected. He was also in the running for the local Council elections I believe.'

'I want to clear it for once and all that George Hancox never sexually abused me. I was happiest at the Hancox's that even I stopped bed-wetting,' Jennifer revealed after all these years.

'One day Mom came to me crying saying I would be going to another family. I was shocked. When Dad came back from work, I was blank. I had no idea why I was being taken away from the family I was so happy with,' says Jennifer.

She would now find another home in Battle Creek, Michigan, for another shot at 'being happy'. This time round with Blaine and Janelle Edgell. This was around the end of 1991.

Dr Randall Haugen, a counsellor, came to pick Jennifer up from 2546 to take her to Battle Creek.

Soon after, George and Melissa Hancox divorced in 1992.

❧

In November 2009, Investigator Michael Rundles was hired by the law firm James Marsh to look into Jennifer's adoption and citizenship papers soon after she was deported. Rundles located George Hancox at his residence at 228 Drew Lane in Athens, Jackson County, Georgia. He was single. According to Hancox, he had hired a lawyer to process Jennifer's papers through the Federal building in Atlanta when Jennifer was with them, and it took a year for her to get her green card and two to get US citizenship. The reason he gave away Jennifer to 'a family in Battle Creek who adopts coloured children with a troubled past' is because Jennifer had a problem getting along with females, like his wife, Melissa. Since his divorce he had no contact with Melissa but heard she lived in California.

Rundles ran up a blank wall as far as Melissa was concerned. She remained untraceable.

❧

There is a very interesting fact from the investigation report dated 12 November 2009, which Private Investigator Rundles wrote under Southern Professional Investigations' firm assigned by Jennifer's US law firm, James Marsh. It read:

> Hancox and his ex-wife, Melissa Johnson Hancox, adopted Jennifer from India in 1990. She was eight years of age. Her mother had tuberculosis and had died. Jennifer was a citizen of India. She was brought to the US by a family, names unknown, whose job was to transport children from foreign countries to the US. The Hancoxes went to the Atlanta airport and picked Jennifer up. A social worker, name unknown, accompanied them.
>
> The adoption was handled through a Lutheran church in Lilburn and the American Embassy in Bombay, India. The Lutheran church may have used an adoption agency. Hancox

hired an attorney in Gwinnett County, last name McBride, to handle the adoption for him. McBride's husband was a judge in Gwinnett County.

McBride handled the paperwork for the adoption through the Federal building in Atlanta. Jennifer was adopted by Hancox and took his last name. It took about 1 year for Jennifer to get a green card and almost 2 years for her to become a US citizen. She did not have a passport. Jennifer attended ESL classes in Gwinnett County and went to Benefield Elementary School in Lawrenceville.

The first paragraph states that Jennifer's mother 'had tuberculosis and had died', which was completely false. This is what Clarice had made the Hancoxes believe, though in reality Wilma was very much alive. This goes to show Clarice's involvement in illegally trafficking Jennifer out of the country by forcefully taking her away from her parents.

But the most important fact that comes to light is in the last paragraph. It mentions:

It took one year for Jennifer to get a green card and almost two years for her to become a US citizen.

Now the big question is, even if she did not have a passport, it still made her a US citizen. If so, where are the papers? Were they lost in transit? Or, did Jennifer and her lawyers overlook this point in Rundell's report? Because if she did get her US citizenship, then it must be somewhere in the files. And if so, then this opens a whole new can of worms! Or should I say, Pandora's box?

22.

Battle Creek is a city in the state of Michigan at the confluence of the Kalamazoo and Battle Creek rivers. It is also nicknamed 'Cereal

City' as it is the headquarters for numerous cereal companies such as Post Cereals, Ralston Cereal Food Factory, and is the home of the ultimate tourist attraction Kellogg's Cereal City USA.

Since 1956, Battle Creek or Cereal City celebrates the world's Longest Breakfast Table Festival, thereby honouring the most important meal of the day—breakfast. People from all over the US as well as other countries visit Cereal City. A breakfast of cereal and milk is served to more than 70,000 tourists during the cereal festival, followed by parades and cultural activities to highlight the city's varied past.

Jennifer remembers going to the cereal festival annually and having a free run of all the yummiest of cereals. 'It was usually held over two days during the weekend in June every year and the tables were spread over Michigan Avenue in downtown Battle Creek. There were music shows, road shows, pageants…it was like a carnival…it was like the community coming together.'

In February 1990, Jennifer entered the US and on 10 May 1991, her adoption was finalized by the Superior Court of Gwinnett County by the Hancoxes. Almost a year later, she was entrusted to the care of AIAA under the supervision of McNitt, who arranged for her placement with the Edgell family in Battle Creek, Michigan. In 1992, Jennifer was formally adopted yet again.

So, Jennifer Francis from Ambernath moved to Lawrenceville as Jennifer Hancox and then onward to Battle Creek as Jennifer Ann Edgell. Quite a journey for a ten year old. But more was yet to come.

On a wintry afternoon Blaine and Janelle Edgell along with their son Jay, came to pick up Jennifer from the Hancox home. There were a few clothes she carried but the two most prized items she took with her to Michigan was her soft toy rabbit Fluffy and her Barbie House set. Jennifer did not understand much at the time nor did she care to but remembers staying at a hotel in Atlanta that night and then driving for a couple of days and nights to Battle Creek in Michigan. It was snowing heavily when the Edgells reached their home with the little girl. 'I was thrilled seeing all the snow around and immediately started making a snowman,' Jennifer's eyes gleam with delight. She had never seen snow before, and recalls, 'I was most amazed.'

There were already four boys living there—three of them were adopted and the eldest, 16-year-old Adam, was their biological son. James 16, Steven 13, and the youngest, Jay, 10 who was of the same age as Jennifer, were biological siblings. They were removed from their mother for abuse.

95 N, Wabash Avenue, the Edgells' home was painted in a light brown colour with a darker shade around the edges. There was a porch, which was later turned into a room, from where one entered the sitting room. Everything was in dark wood. On the left was the living room with a TV and Blaine's lounge chair and to the right was the dining room with a big table, a china cabinet, and a piano. None of these areas were walled, except a door to the left that led to the kitchen. Another door led to the backyard, which had a swing set, a garage and a patio. There were two huge greyhounds, Jennifer remembers. Her room was done up in blue with a canopy bed.

Blaine Edgell was a fair, dark-blonde haired and blue-eyed handsome man. He used to fix windows and provide utility services and worked in a firm called Lumber besides having his own private business. A local Battle Creek boy, his mother lived 15 minutes away from his house.

To celebrate Jennifer's homecoming, Blaine had taken the family along with some churchgoers (he was an active church member) to Pizza Hut.

His wife, Janelle Lynn, was herself an adopted child by the Poysers, a jolly set of people. The Poysers would drop by and play

Bingo with the family. Every Saturday and Sunday, the Edgell children would visit their Poyser grandparents who would spoil them with ice cream and popcorn. Janelle had long dark brown hair and was very old-fashioned and a bit of a prude. Jennifer's recurring memory of her was of sewing clothes.

The Edgell children, including Jennifer, were home-schooled mainly by Janelle, who was compensated by the government for taking in children with difficult backgrounds and home-schooling them. Classes were mainly conducted in the basement, which was huge and divided into three sections: one housing a video games room, one had the laundry (which included a shute for throwing clothes from the second floor to the laundry room), and the third was the home-school room. Sometimes classes were taken upstairs while Janelle sewed. 'She was a lousy teacher though. She would make us stand and read and teach us to rattle out the names of all the US presidents. That is one thing I can do right away,' says Jennifer. 'She would be paid by the government for home-schooling us but all we mostly did were household chores. She would make us clean all the cracks in the house with a toothbrush and write different chores for us everyday. She made us feel it was part of the curriculum. Bitch. And she was very strict. We barely studied for two hours, and cleaned the house and did housework for the rest of the time.'

'We were treated a little better than slaves. Till someone told on the Edgells and we were sent to school. Janelle's home-schooling funds also stopped,' grins Jennifer wickedly.

A couple of months after Jennifer was with the Edgells, another set of abandoned siblings, Fatiha 14, JR 11 and Shay 7 joined the Edgell brood. 'Fatiha and me became great friends and we are in touch till date. I was shifted out of my room and shared a room with Fatiha, as part of the front porch was converted to our room,' recalls Jennifer. Fatiha was the only one who went to school. She went to South West High and was a good looking and popular chic. However she suffered from a peculiar bone disease.

'I am in touch with Fatiha. We also call her Tia. She stays in Wisconsin and works in stores and has a son, Talique, out of wedlock.'

A couple of months later a six-month-old baby, Tiffany, joined them. 'Her mom had thrown her in the garbage. She was real cute though she was a cry baby,' says Jennifer. 'She however has no hair till date.'

Ten houses from 95 Wabash lived a family with whose children the Edgell brood was friendly. They played and went swimming together. One evening Janelle and Blaine went out leaving Adam in charge of the children at the neighbours. Adam pinned Jennifer down and started fondling and kissing her for 15 minutes or so till he was told to 'lay off' by the neighbour's boy Shaun. When Jennifer complained to Janelle, the first thing she got from her foster mother was a resounding slap on her face for 'lying'. 'Janelle was awfully scared of Blaine who abused her also from time to time. I was told she died in 2012. Poor lady though a thorough bitch,' says Jennifer.

The second time round she was abused was when Steven was playing with her Barbie set and making obscene gestures with Ken and Barbie. When Jennifer complained to Blaine, he beat her up 'with a belt' and told her there was nothing 'abnormal' about that. Blaine would beat the children on a whim. 'He was a good-looking man and exuded a lot of power. We were scared man to complain against him. Nobody would believe us,' says Jennifer. 'And worse, Janelle was too scared of him. That fat lazy cow.'

Apart from Adam and Steven, Blaine had also started abusing Jennifer. At eleven her breasts were beginning to develop and she started her periods. For some strange reason, Blaine was partial to Fatiha and rude to Jennifer. He shifted Jennifer to the attic, next to the boys' rooms so that he could have easy access to abuse her. They shared a common bath without a lock on the door and Jennifer out of sheer fright of being abused refused to bathe for days on end. Finally, the government sent a letter to the Edgells to send the children to a special needs' school. A college girl was assigned to help bathe Jennifer and introduced her to music. 'I learnt to rap and hip hop.'

One evening, there was no one other than Jennifer and Blaine at home. The boys had gone to play at the neighbours' and Janelle had taken the girls out to the supermarket. Jennifer was not feeling well. She was playing a Nintendo game in the video room.

'Hey girl, come. Sit on Dad's lap, Dad's little darling,' Blaine asked Jennifer. She wondered why this sudden change of attitude towards her. As she hesitantly came and sat on his lap, Blaine Edgell started to fondle her tiny breasts and pinching them. Jennifer felt something was not quite right. She had the urge to run but Blaine held her back.

When she managed to tear herself from Blaine's clutches, she ran as fast as her little legs could take her, straight to Shaun's where her brothers were playing. They had not seen her as she stood at the corner of their garden panting. 'I was scared to go there also. Steven and Adam would make fun of me…' she breaks off. From the frying pan into the fire?

It was almost six months since the video room episode with Blaine took place. Jennifer told no one and Blaine had not misbehaved since then.

One Sunday afternoon the family were heading to the Willard Beach Public Park by the city's largest lake, the Goguac Lake. Fatiha helped by Janelle had made pretty short dresses for the three girls—Jennifer, Shay and Tiffany. There was a big family reunion, and all cousins from either side of the family were assembling. While the children were playing by themselves, the adults were playing baseball. Blaine got hit by the ball and had a mild concussion. Janelle dropped him home along with Jennifer saying, 'Jennifer be a good daughter and take care of your father. We will be back home soon.'

'Yes,' Jennifer nodded though a little apprehensive.

Fifteen minutes later, Blaine called out to Jennifer. 'Honey, get me a glass of water,' lying in the bed in his room. As Jennifer gave him the water, he started to fondle her and touched her all over. When Jennifer began to cringe, he suddenly exclaimed, 'Oh bull. I thought you were Janelle. You remind me so much of her.' He grinned evilly. Like the devil incarnate though he kept up his public appearance as he was also a standby pastor in the local Christian Fellowship Church.

'Hiya,' Jennifer yelled as she skipped into the house one afternoon from school. It was unusually quiet in there that afternoon. 'Is anybody home?'

'Yes darling, I'm home,' Blaine returned as he got up from his lounge chair walking up to her. Jennifer's heart skipped a beat seeing the evil grin on his face.

'Where's mom?' she stuttered.

'Why do you need mom when Daddy is here darling,' Blaine laughed.

Before Jennifer could run, Blaine caught her, tied her to a pole on the basement, slapped her and before she knew, he was on her, having sex with her. She had no idea what was going on but felt 'pain as something was penetrating my body. I was in shock and fear.' This was her first sexual encounter.

From then on it was a never-ending process. He would force himself on her whenever he would get her alone…in the attic, in the basement, on the couch. Three or four times a week Blaine would force Jennifer into having sex with him. Every time he abused her, he would apologize and tell her he thought she 'was his wife'. 'How crazy that was' is all Jennifer can say now. Sometimes, it would be painful intercourse and other times oral sex. She was repulsed but had no choice. And, none to confide in.

One day she confided in Fatiha. Instead of helping her out, 'That c*nt told me to rinse my mouth with mouthwash,' Jennifer bursts out after all these years.

One a particular Wednesday night, Jennifer did not go to church as she was feeling ill. She had not gone to school too. When everyone was away, he took her to the basement and tied her to the pole again. This time he put a broomstick inside her till Jennifer screamed in pain. He then tried putting a hot dog inside her and finally had anal sex that left the little girl scarred for life. This would be repeated over and over again, and many a time when Janelle questioned Blaine about Jennifer's injuries, he would blame it on the boys, especially Jay and say it was an accident while playing.

'I told a couple of people about what was happening. I told my sister Fatiha, two people in the Church and my cousins Jennifer and Jessica Rathe (from Blaine's side), but nobody helped me. I even told the Pastor in the Church but nobody wanted to believe me because of Blaine's influence in the community.'

By then Jennifer was attending Springfield Elementary School, with her cousins Jennifer (Jen) and Jessica (Jess). It was during the sex education class that Jennifer first realized what was happening to her. 'That's how I found out what sex was and what is good and what is bad.' One day Jennifer told her principal about Blaine's behaviour. She immediately alerted the school counsellor Randy Hogan. He along with a social worker, Vicki, after going through Jennifer's complaints showed her dolls and asked her what happened. After she described what was happening at home, she was removed from the Edgell's home the very same day. The other children remained there.

The police came and arrested Blaine and put him away in a lock-up for a night. Janelle was furious with Jennifer because it meant a loss of face in the community. She blamed Jennifer of lying.

However, she was taken out from the Edgell's and put in a foster home in Marshall, about 20 minutes from Battle Creek.

Though Jennifer was happy at the Edgell's, she was having nightmares because of Blaine's sexual abuses. She started bed-wetting again.

※

The next day Vicki took her for a medical examination at Ann Arbor Hospital. 'After the examination I overheard someone saying that I had been badly damaged inside and I would never be able to have children. I was just into my teens. I was devastated. I don't know if I was pregnant or not, but they told me that my uterus had been cleaned. Am sure there must be some records somewhere in the hospital about this,' says Jennifer.

Later Jennifer met Blaine outside the courtroom when they were brought face to face and he apologized to her. He was sent for six months of counselling.

'I later learnt,' says Jennifer, 'that Blaine along with the boys Adam, Steven and James all eventually became convicted sex offenders and could not be around children. Years later, Adam was charged with abusing his own daughters and James received a life sentence.'

※

Though living with the Edgells had become a nightmare in the last few months of her three years stay with them, Jennifer who calls herself 'Jennifer Edgell Haynes', still credits some of her happiest childhood memories to them.

For the first time since her birth and her earliest childhood memories, she felt she belonged to a family. And to a community. The Edgells were well-respected in Battle Creek. Her best memories are that of Christmas at the Edgell's home. Janelle used to make coffee cakes on Christmas eve, and everybody would come down at four in the morning to collect their gifts. Blaine would always give common family gifts such as a treadmill or a gaming console. Uncles and aunts would give individual gifts. Play dough, Barbie sets, a bike and new clothes are some of the gifts Jennifer remembers receiving. Grandparents from both sides of the family would come down for brunch to their home armed with more gifts. During the day, Blaine and the boys could be found watching football. Blaine's favourite team was the American Cowboys. There would be egg salads, hotdogs and cheese for brunch, followed by a fancy dinner party with turkey and dressing.

One of Jennifer's favourite food was Aunty Shelley's Rice—a handed-down recipe, most likely from a great aunt called Shelley from Janelle's side of the family. Hence the name Aunty Shelley's Rice. It was a special rice dish baked with onion juice, lemon juice and chicken. 'I did try and make the rice here once. It turned out pretty good though I did not have the correct onion juice. Fatiha has the recipe and she does a damn good job of it. Am waiting to go back and have Fatiha make it for me,' smiles Jennifer.

Apart from the weekend popcorn, ice cream and karaoke nights at grandparent Poysers', there was the great Cereal Festival to look forward to annually. 'We used to have an annual Block Party. Everyone in the neighbourhood got food and we all shared a potluck while getting to know each other. Those were good memories. There was a feel of belonging to a community,' Jennifer reminisces.

The saddest moment of her life was when the Edgells gave up their rights on Jennifer in the court in front of the judge, and Janelle blamed Jennifer for 'Blaine's behaviour and wrecking her marriage.'

As Jennifer puts it, 'I was very very upset and cried for years. At that moment my whole life changed. I did not give a fuck about anything anymore.'

23.

George and Melissa Hancox's adoption of Jennifer was finalized by the Superior Court of Gwinnett County on 10 May 1991. The Honorable Justice Bryant Huff passed the following order:

> The parental rights of the biological father and mother have been terminated and that George and Melissa Hancox shall have the permanent custody of the said minor child, Jennifer, and that the child shall have a right of inheritance as provided by the law and the name of the minor child is hereby changed to Jennifer Marie Hancox.

But a year later, the Hancoxes contacted AIAA (the agency that facilitated Jennifer's adoption) to remove Jennifer from the family on account of her 'difficult behaviour'. She was entrusted to an AIAA employee, Myrna McNitt, for supervision. It was McNitt who arranged for Jennifer's placement with the Edgell family in Michigan, who formally adopted her in 1992.

McNitt, whose supervisory period of Jennifer was extended, sent in her report to Tom Black, the Protective Services Supervisor of Calhoun County Department of Social Services on 7 October 1993.

In her report, she states:

> During the course of my supervision with the Edgells, Jennifer disclosed that George Hancox would take her for camping trips alone without other adults or children...and play 'bed games' with her. I was informed about this by a relative of George's.
>
> In January 1992, the Edgells reported sexual contact between Jay, Steven, James and Jennifer...mainly exposing and mutual touching of each other's genitals...where Jennifer was the

aggressor especially with Steven, sexually and in other ways...

The Edgells reported all the sexual activities between the children...in order to set in the necessary safeguards for their family.

Throughout the course of my supervision with the Edgells... they talked about home-schooling and the need for therapy...I personally found them to be cooperative and nurturing of their children...and found the home-schooling to be a benefit to Jennifer...however she was a 'flitter' though the Edgells showed a tremendous perseverance with Jennifer.

In conclusion...at no point did I feel they were not acting in Jennifer's best interest. I would not hesitate to place another child with the Edgells.

If we look at the above reports by McNitt, we see how at every point, she contradicts what Jennifer's memories are of the Hancoxes and Edgells. As we saw earlier, Jennifer completely denies having been abused by George. In fact, she reiterates that she had the best time with George and Melissa and her bed-wetting had stopped completely. She also admits she was a difficult child and accepts that she behaved badly with Melissa. She agrees she may have said something about being sexually abused by George, but that was 'after being brainwashed and forced to by the Edgells'. Jennifer feels McNitt's reports were completely 'doctored at the behest of the Edgells as Blaine was a powerful man'.

'It's all bloody lies,' is all Jennifer says. 'That bitch instead of helping me, messed up my life big time. She put me from the frying pan straight into the fire. Hope she burns in hell.'

※

According to information sourced from the Internet, McNitt's expertise ranges in the field of child protection and welfare, foster care, adoption and juvenile justice. Apart from working as a caseworker for over three decades for AIAA and serving at the Circuit Court Family Division in Michigan, McNitt served as a faculty member at the Grand Valley State University. She also served as a Clinical Supervisor for several international programmes, including, Dominican social work in Guatemala as well as Feed the Children in Kenya, Haiti and the UK.

In 2004, the Family Independence Agency (FIA) along with the Michigan state authorities raided McNitt's home and office and seized records showing her organization—Michigan Foster and Adoptive Parent Association (MFAPA)—of embezzling millions of dollars of state funds. One of her former financial director, Gerald Maat resigned saying, 'I had no access to the group's financial papers as all records were hidden and one had no idea how the money was acquired or was being spent.' McNitt herself was accused of embezzling state funds under the garb of social work.

It is a strange coincidence that the key people associated with the adoption of Jennifer (and possibly several others like her)—Clarice D'Souza from the Kuan Yin Charitable Trust as well as Jodie Darragh and Myrna McNitt from AIAA—have all been caught on the wrong side of the law.

Does this make it an accidental coincidence or a deliberate coincidence?

And is inter-country adoption a garb for child trafficking?

Much remains to be seen in this regard, and we will attempt to get a clearer view in the subsequent chapters.

24.

Once out of the Edgell's home, Jennifer was put into a foster home in Marshall about 20 minutes away from Battle Creek. She attended the same school with cousins Jen and Jess Rathe but did not enjoy her stay with her new foster family at Marshall.

After less than a fortnight's stay at her new home, Jennifer ran away to Battle Creek. She just hung around with Jen and Jess doing nothing much till she finally gave herself in. Since Calhoun County was full up with juvenile matters, her case was transferred to Star Commonwealth in Albion City in Michigan.

The social worker assigned to Jennifer here was a man named Alan, who put her in a foster home in Albion with an African American family called the Presleys. The home was run by an old lady called Caroline Presley whose granddaughter, Monica, befriended her, and they started hanging around together. She was now sent to a special school in Star Commonwealth where she met up with her sister Fatiha. Fatiha was expelled from Southwest High as she was caught belting a girl there.

Caroline, like most foster care parents, spent very little on the children of the money she received for their welfare. She hardly bought them any clothes and the food was dismal. Nevertheless, Jennifer stayed with the Presleys for almost a year. The main reason was Monica. They would sneak out over the weekends with boys and go out for parties and get gifts and food from them. 'I enjoyed myself during that time. It was a lot of freedom and a lot of fun. Especially after the strict rules at the Edgells,' she says.

Jennifer was a difficult child given her tormented childhood and dysfunctional adoptive homes. She was rude, rough, disobedient and refused to adjust. She deliberately refused to follow hygiene methods and adjust in foster care or at her adoptive homes. Even as a child, she refused to be pinned down to a routine due to which her schooling remained inconsistent and irregular. She enjoyed being on the run, hustling and stealing, rather than thinking of the future or a career.

When she talks, her normal language is full of slangs and cuss words. She cannot say two sentences, even today, without swearing. She peppers her sentences with slangs as if they are mere adverbs and adjectives!

Jennifer was also in the habit of using her hands, nails and teeth to fight if things did not go her way. If verbal abuse did not work, she would resort to physical violence. It was her way of defending herself from her childhood days or expressing her frustration at life. This behaviour, though well under control now, still surfaces once in a while.

Some months ago, I had given Jennifer some clothes. En route home on the train, a passenger jostled her as he was getting into the train. The bag of clothes slipped from her hand but Jennifer managed to grab the man and 'bite his ears hard' before the train took off. The man was obviously either too shocked or in too much pain to react to Jennifer's behaviour. 'But, how could you Jenny?' I asked shocked. 'You just don't bite anyone like that.'

'Serves the son of a b**ch right. He deserved it,' Jennifer said matter-of-factly completely ignoring my question. Then smiling mischievously she added, 'It's been quite a while since I bit someone.'

Jennifer herself admits she was difficult not because she wanted to be difficult but she was generally very angry with life and with everyone around her. While at the Edgells, she was especially angry with Janelle, because she considered her as her 'mom' and 'as a mom she totally neglected our needs,' says Jennifer. 'Apart from treating us like slaves and making us do housework instead of studying, she also knew Blaine was sexually abusing us and let that pass. I refused to bathe for days on end; I would slam doors; I would lock myself in my room for hours, and at times I would deliberately pee in the bed so that Janelle had a lot more laundry to do.'

Jennifer recollects the time she got her periods at eleven years. Although Janelle had taught her how to use sanitary napkins, she deliberately left a trail of blood all over for Janelle to clean.

Over the next few years until she was eighteen, Jennifer changed fifty foster homes, staying at various places for as long as twenty-four months to as briefly as twenty-four hours!

'The next few years were a blur,' Jennifer admits. 'I drifted through foster homes and group homes. I would run away from the homes and always be brought back either to the homes or to remand homes. The reason that I kept running away was that none of the families seemed to ever care for me. They were only interested in the money they got from the government for having me. All I wanted was a home where I could love and be loved.'

In and out of foster homes, erratic school attendance and with no one to enforce any discipline in her life, the next most obvious step for the teenager was to get into wrong company and develop wrong habits.

The first time she did weed—a type of drug using Cannabis leaves—was when she was around 15. Before that she had smoked a joint once when she was 11 but that was more for a lark. She was living at Marshall in the Projects, which is basically a crime-infested low-income group area. She befriended two sisters her age, 'one was fat and one was thin.' They all bunked school and went to the duo's house and smoked up. The sisters were already doing weed. The first time Jennifer felt a buzz in her head and later when she returned home, she ate like a pig, 'cleaned all the chicken, cheese macaroni Caroline [Presley] made,' and slept like a baby.

Jennifer liked the experience so much that she repeated it in the next few days, little realizing that she was getting addicted to it. She skipped school and smoked weed.

Her school complained to Caroline who in turn put her in a juvenile home in Marshall. But Jennifer escaped after a couple of days. After staying with a friend for a few days and 'doing more weed,' she turned herself in. She was then put in another foster care in Jackson, a city between Ann Arbor and Lansing and known as the birthplace of the Republican Party.

Since most of her foster parents never bothered to buy her proper clothes or necessities, Jennifer started going out with a lot of African American boys who bought her gifts, took her out to restaurants and parties and bought her weed. 'But they were just casual flings, nothing serious,' she smiles.

'Weed was easy to smoke up and cheaper than cocaine, heroin and other stuff. Besides, it was less harmful and less addictive than cocaine or heroin. It gave a buzz, just what I needed to forget my horrible circumstances. It also gave me the guts to go and do things which otherwise I would hesitate to do,' says Jennifer.

Around this time Jennifer also started shoplifting. 'Since the foster care folks never looked after us well, we would gang up together and steal clothes and shoes from stores like Meijer's and K Mart,' Jennifer admits nonchalantly. 'Jackson was a very big and very nice city. I had a lot of fun there. A few times I stole from K Mart and managed to escape. Once I got caught and was put in juvenile prison. But I managed to escape after a few days.'

And that is how Jennifer's teenage years came to be determined. Changing foster homes, doing drugs, stealing, getting into juvenile homes, escaping, being put into another home and another. An endless rigmarole.

'I didn't give a shit about life. Since my life was one big shit. All I did was live for the moment. Live on the edge.'

Jennifer was always on the run. Especially from the foster homes, schools and juvenile homes. Sometimes, she would not adhere to the discipline of a particular home, or be rude or disappear for days or simply pick up fights with other residents.

In one of the reports by a social worker, she was caught 'engaging in a sexual act with one of the children' which was described as 'unusual sexual act'. Jennifer obviously denies it. 'Nope. Never had those tendencies. In fact, I was disgusted with sex and sexual intercourse having gone through what I did at the Edgells. I hated the word, and I was more scared to engage in it because sex to me was "dirty" and associated with pain.'

One is not sure whether this is true or not—whether reports by the social worker were doctored or not, just like Jennifer claimed 'George Hancox's sexual abuse' was doctored. Or perhaps Jennifer deliberately chose not to remember. Or maybe she really did not remember given the fact she was 'mostly on weed and totally screwed up'. Or for Jennifer having gone through so much of sexual abuse, these acts seemed normal to her.

Meanwhile like all teenagers, especially the ones on their own, Jennifer hung around with boys and had her share of boyfriends.

The first boy she ever had a crush on was a white American boy called Chad Moody whom she met in the Church while she was with the Edgells. Jennifer says she really liked him, and he also reciprocated as he used to smile back at her from the pews. But, it did not go beyond the smiles. 'That was my first crush,' Jennifer smiles.

One of the foster homes she was placed in was at Karen Rathe's in Battle Creek at 100 Lethrop. Karen was related to Blaine by marriage. Karen's brother was married to Blaine's sister. 'I liked Aunt Karen's place and got along well with my cousins, her daughters. One of the best times I had at foster care was at her place.'

'Aunt Karen had three daughters, Jennifer, Jessica and Leah. I went to school with Jen and Jess the older two. Then there was the Bozell family, African American, with a single father and his four boys. Karen was dating the father and Jen and Jess dated the two older boys. I don't remember their names, but all their names started with Q,' she recollects.

The third boy Quentin was interested in Jennifer while the

youngest Bozell, Quincy, was dating the youngest of the Rathe sisters, Leah. The Bozell boys would come and have dinner and watch TV with the Rathe girls and hang out with them. They were however not allowed to go up to the bedrooms. 'Aunt Karen kept her relationship with Bozell pretty discreet,' discloses Jennifer.

Quentin was already dating someone when Jennifer came in with the Rathes. He started showing interest in Jennifer. Jennifer was a little hesitant at first but gave in. 'I liked his smile. It was gentle.' Quentin soon split up from his girlfriend and started seeing Jennifer. Initially, apart from dinner and TV at home they would go to the park or for a movie. They mostly held hands and kissed. 'My thing was not boys then. All I was into was making money. Besides, I was not comfortable with sex. I was scared. Sex to me was something painful.'

'Quentin was gentle and asked my permission whether we could have sex. I cried and told him my horrible experiences. He understood and explained to me that sex was to be enjoyed and should not be a painful experience. I was surprised because he was the first man who asked for my permission to have sex with me. No one had ever done that before. He was the first guy whom I let go all the way.'

'I was with Quentin Bozell for nearly a year.'

In the meantime Jennifer managed to complete her 10th grade and enrolled into the 11th grade in Battle Creek High School. But, she was not consistent in school. She would frequently slip out of school to smoke up and steal clothes, shoes and food items from stores and super markets, like Meijer's, JC Penny, Sears, K Mart and other such places.

Soon, she dropped out of school altogether. Life was now all about living on the edge.

25.

Of all the fifty foster homes Jennifer moved in and out in her six odd years, Karen Rathe's (in Battle Creek) and Caroline Presley's (in Albion) homes were the longest she lived at and were her most memorable stays. This was despite her irrational behaviour there. It was during her days at the Presleys' that Jennifer started doing weed and shoplifting, as Caroline seldom spent the welfare funds on her. She was erratic in school and in and out of juvenile homes. Finally, she managed to run away from the foster care homes and the juvenile homes for a while.

When Jennifer was about eighteen years old, she befriended a twenty-seven-year-old single African American girl called Teresa and stayed with her at Jackson, a 'big and nice city' she 'really digs'. They started stealing at the local K Mart and once she was caught but was let off after a warning.

Jackson had a predominantly African American population. Sixty per cent of the citizens in Jackson were Black. Jackson was also a rough city, where lot of crimes happened. According to Jennifer, 'The chicks in Jackson were really really rough.'

Meijer's is a chain of stores found mainly in the states of Michigan, Illinois, Indiana and Kentucky, dealing in groceries, apparels, home goods and electronics. The largest Meijer's outlet in Jackson was near Michigan Avenue and open round the clock. Jennifer used to hang around smoking weed, and occasionally indulge in petty theft from the store. There was a mixed race girl called Toya who sometimes hung around smoking up with Jennifer outside Meijer's.

'Hey, wanna jam with us babe?' Toya asked Jennifer one day as she stubbed a cigarette under her boots outside Meijer's. Toya was tall, slim with fake platinum blonde locks falling over her shoulders. She was of mixed parentage—half white American, quarter African American and a quarter Mexican.

'Yeah. Sure man. What do you want me to do?' Jennifer asked.

'Here. Come with me,' Toya led her into her car, a metallic blue Chevrolet. 'Get in.'

Jennifer met up with two African American boys who were in their early twenties. Toya was in her late teens. All of them were much older than the skinny Jennifer, who looked younger than her sixteen years. And she was horribly thin. The boys were Derrick and Brandon. Toya's family was well-off. She had money and a car and decided to 'drive around for fun and see the world' in her Chevvy. They had a chat with Jennifer who seemed quite excited. 'Hey girl. You be careful and get this right. If this is successful then you can come along with us and have fun. Get me?' Toya asked.

'Gotcha.' Jennifer replied.

The modus operandi was this. Brandon stayed in the car, ready at the wheels to take off quickly. Derrick stood in front of the store, smoking casually. Toya and Jennifer went into the store and took a whole lot of clothes for trial. They went into the changing room and kept wearing tee shirts or shirts or dresses and trousers and jeans, one over the other. Toya had a security sensor remover which she used to remove the security sensors so they did not beep as they left the store. Meanwhile, they wore enough clothes so as not to look too fat and yet be able to walk comfortably. If some sensors could not be removed, they just left the clothes in the changing room. Then Toya and Jennifer walked out and got into the car. Derrick joined them after making sure no one suspected or followed them. Once the trio were in the car, Brandon drove off.

'Whew!' Jennifer giggled. 'That was cool!'

'Welcome to the Chevvy Chase Gang,' Toya put out her hand out to Jennifer, who held and shook it.

'I like it man. I like it. Chevvy Chase. That's cool,' said Jennifer. 'Now what the fuck do I do with all these clothes man? I feel like a friggin' Santa Claus.'

'Just hang in there for a bit, will you?' Toya replied.

After driving out of the Meijer's store in Jackson and keeping close to the freeway, they stopped at the next Meijer's outlet twenty miles out of the city. A mile before that they stopped at a 7/11 gas station where Toya took Jennifer to the ladies' washroom. She pulled out a huge folded Meijer's carry bag from her handbag and both of them pulled out the clothes they were wearing and put it in the bag. When they reached the next Meijer's outlet, the boys took their old positions while the girls walked into the store and told the lady at the cash counter that they wanted to return the clothes. 'Mommy got them for me. As usual her tastes are lousy. Don't match with mine,' Toya said. 'Just want the money back. No exchange.'

'Okay,' the lady added the total cost and handed Toya the money. 'Here's $425.' Jennifer couldn't help let out a gasp as she had never had such a large haul of stolen goods herself. While Toya was collecting her money, Jennifer managed to slip in a couple of costume necklaces into her pocket.

Once in the car, Toya admonished her. 'Never do that ever. No picking stuff at the counter and slipping in your pocket. You can get caught anytime. Too risky. Everyone's watching, and you could have landed me in trouble.'

'Sorry, man. My fault. Just got a little excited at the sound of so much cash. Won't happen again.'

'Hey, what do we do with all the money?' Jennifer asked.

'We split it equally,' Toya explained the rules of the game. 'And we bear all the costs equally including the gas and the maintenance of the car.'

Five miles ahead they spotted a Sear's outlet. This time it was the boys' turn to visit the store while Toya sat at the wheels and Jennifer kept a look out for their safety. The modus operandi was the same. By six in the evening they were richer by another $245. They split the money and suddenly Jennifer realized she was hungry.

'Hey what about some grub, man? Am hungry. Let's stop at the nearest McD.' 'Yep. We'll pull up ahead. One's five minutes away. Here Jenny, let me explain how we go about here,' Toya explained. 'Listen carefully.'

※

As they neared the McDonald's outlet and parked the car in the lot, the foursome went in. Brandon and Toya stood in two different queues, all the time keeping an eye on the people ahead of them as they placed their order. Meanwhile Derrick led Jennifer to a table for four and waited for the others. 'You're a quick learner Jenny. So tell me about yourself,' Derrick asked.

While the two chatted, Brandon and Toya kept their ears cocked as people ahead of them placed their orders.

'Four cheeseburgers, two large fries, four medium Cokes and one dozen chicken nuggets,' the man in front of Brandon ordered. In the next lane, Toya ordered two cheeseburgers and a large Coke with a large fries. Brandon quietly slipped out of the queue and as the man in front of him with the large order collected his meals and was on his way out, Brandon quietly managed to pull out his bill. As Toya reached the table, Brandon joined her and slipped her the bill.

After waiting for fifteen odd minutes while they shared the fries, Toya got up to go to a different counter and said, 'Look pal. I ordered four cheeseburgers and you gave me two and one Coke less.' Brandon stood behind her quietly glaring at the guy at the counter.

'Let me check, Ma'am,' the young boy replied nervously.

'Look mate, I don't have all the time in the world. Hurry it up will you,' Toya glared.

'Yes…' The boy stuttered as he quickly placed two cheeseburgers and a large Coke with a large fries thrown in. 'Here you go, Ma'am. Sorry for the inconvenience.'

'No sweat,' Toya smiled back.

This was what they did in most of the fast food outlets like

McDonald's, Burger King, KFC, Wendy's and A&B Root Beer. Sometimes, they were recompensed with entire meals. In case they wanted to stop by for a coffee or doughnut, they paid as they thought it was too much of work and too big a risk for a small amount of money.

It was past ten at night when the Chevvy pulled up at Jackson. 'Hey Jenny,' Toya said, 'You can stay with me for the night. Pack a small case with a few clothes and necessities from your place in the morning and we hit the road before lunchtime. Eleven should be fine. And we are not gonna see this place for the next one year. We are gonna travel and shop and eat and live in style.'

'You got it honey,' Brandon pecked Toya on the lips.

'Count me in too pal,' Derrick showed a thumbs-up.

'Me too man. I'm in,' Jennifer smiled.

And this is how the foursome spent a whole year between 1998 and 1999, travelling all over from Michigan to Indiana to Chicago, Wisconsin, Ohio to cities closer to home like Battle Creek and Jackson to Kalamazoo, St Joseph's, Detroit, Fort Wayne and a whole lot of others. They mainly kept to the freeways. Stealing from Meijer's, K Mart, Sears, JC Penny and living off the loot and hoodwinking fast food joints like Burger King, McDonald's, Wendy's and others for free meals. They drove through the day in Toya's blue Chevvy and at night they would check in at motels like Motel 6, Nights Inn, Holiday Inn, Bombay Hotel and others past midnight. Between 1 a.m. and 1 p.m., most of these hotels were let out at half rent. Sometimes, they even managed to gyp the management and stay for free.

On an average, they made between $500 and $600 on a good day. Some days they made no money. On such days they would all chill out in their motel rooms and smoke up. Though Jennifer does not accept it, she and Derrick did have some sort of a relationship going on. As did Toya and Brandon. But, it was an on and off thing. None of the kids took relationships seriously because apart from Toya, all three of them came from very poor backgrounds. The foremost on their minds was to make money. Neither did they take life seriously. They took each day as it came and ate, drank, smoked and made merry. For them life was all about living on the edge, and they were hedonists in the true sense of the term.

One afternoon when Jennifer was at the Meijer's store in Jackson having wrapped herself in several layers of clothing, she felt the white security man's eyes on her. Previously, she had had a record in Lansing for misdemeanour and had served some time in a juvenile home. Perhaps, the authorities were wizening up on the four and their activities, and had their photographs on their records.

As she stepped out, Jennifer did the stupidest thing possible. She pulled out a bar of chocolate and started to eat it without having paid for it. The security guard whose eyes were glued to Jennifer did not let this opportunity slip. He immediately called to her, 'Please step aside Miss.'

'Why man? What did I do?' Jennifer tried to sound cool though she was nervous as hell from the inside.

'You haven't paid for the chocolate Miss,' he said.

'Oh that. Sorry dude. I was hungry. I'll just pay. My fault,' she smiled.

As she unzipped her wallet, the security man saw a tag hanging from behind her back. He immediately called out to his lady colleague, 'Hey Penny. Come here. Please check this Miss here.'

Before Jennifer could put up a protest she was led away to the changing room by Penny and out came the stolen clothes. Scared at what was in store for her, Jennifer started to cry. 'Alright,' the security guy said as he punched her name on the computer and her previous record of misdemeanour popped up, 'Here Miss. I am letting you go. But here, keep this,' he said as he handed her a slip of paper. 'You will have to appear in court on this given date here,' he said pointing at the paper. Jennifer nodded as she left crying.

As luck would have it Jennifer missed the court date. A warrant was issued in her name that she was on the run. It was nearly a year since the four were out on the road. Besides, Jennifer's warrant did not make matters easy. So a year after they started out, the Chevvy Chase Gang decided to split. Each took their share of the booty and went their way.

Jennifer and Derrick decided to head out together. Derrick was already hustling i.e. selling drugs. They both decided to hustle together. And, thus started a new phase in Jennifer's life.

Derrick took Jennifer to a house in Jackson that was full of crackheads. There are essentially two kinds of addicts. One who like taking drugs as part of their lifestyle but have other means of employment to fund their addiction. They dope to live. The other lot live to dope. They steal, mug, kill just so as to fund their addiction. The latter are known as crackheads.

The life of a crackhead is very different from a businessman or a lawyer or a professional drug addict. They usually have no immediate employers, are always shabbily turned out, living in run-down neighbourhoods with bad hygiene, especially dental. The front few teeth are always missing due to consumption of crack and their language is peppered with slangs.

The ground floor of the building was full of crackheads snorting while the first floor had the hustlers or dealers as they are called. On the top floor, the hustlers and homeless slept.

Jennifer bought a gun under the table; a .45 colt for $20. She did not know how to use it but at 17 she kept it strapped to her trousers as she hustled to keep her body and soul together. She and Derrick went to homeless shelters to eat. But, after a few weeks of hustling,

Jennifer got tired and decided to go back to Detroit.

She befriended a girl called Tania and stayed with her for some time. Tania helped get her a 'work only' social security card with the number 256774065. Meanwhile, Tania's grandmother told her to get her immigration papers in order and offered to help her with it, but Jennifer did not realize its importance and did not bother to follow it up.

At the time, Jennifer was nearing eighteen when she decided to go back to Karen Rathe or Aunt Karen. She had had a fall out with her earlier as she had pushed her roughly over some argument. Though some bad blood had flowed between them, Karen let her stay with her for some time. She loved being with Jen and Jess, and Quentin drifted in and out of her life.

26.

Through all this time, while Jennifer changed two adoptive homes and several foster homes, neither the private nor the public child welfare agencies took any action to finalize Jennifer's US citizenship. This was because Jennifer did not qualify for the automatic citizenship under the Child Citizenship Act passed in 2000. Instead, she remained merely a Lawful Permanent Resident, and thereby subject to removal.

George Hancox did file an application with the United States Citizenship and Immigration Services (USCIS) requesting Jennifer's citizenship, but this application lapsed when Jennifer was removed from the Hancox home. USCIS sent three letters to Hancox and her application was denied when she failed to appear at three successive interview appointments.

In a letter dated 15 October 1992, Thomas Fischer the District Director writes:

On January 16, 1992, April 27, 1992 and September 8, 1992, you were scheduled to appear for an examination on your application for naturalization, which was filed in accordance with Section 322(a) of the Immigration and Nationality Act. You did not appear and have failed to notify this office of any reason why you were unable to keep the appointment.

It is noted that you may be eligible to apply for naturalization again on or after September 12, 1992.

Hancox returned this letter to the USCIS with the comment 'Lives in Michigan', and the envelope is marked 'Left No Address'.

When Jennifer started living with the Edgells in Battle Creek, Blaine and Janelle applied to formally adopt her in the Calhoun County Probate Court. On 22 December 1992, she was finally adopted by them.

However, after being adopted by the Edgells, Jennifer did not stay on long enough with them for them to apply for her US citizenship. She was removed from 95 N Wabash and lived in and out of various foster care homes.

Documents in the Freedom of Information Act (FOIA) file indicate that at least one of her foster families agreed to follow up on her citizenship. But, it seems no further action was taken in this regard. Thus, Jennifer continued to be a citizen of India and a Lawful Permanent Resident of the US, thereby subject to removal at any given time.

Little Jenny with her mother, Wilma, before being trafficked out of the country

Jenny in the US soon after her adoption

Justin and Jennifer with toddler Kadafi and baby Kassana

Jennifer with her children, Kassana and Kadafi, as she left them in the US

Judy Cobbs with Kadafi and Kassana

Jennifer at work at a call centre in Mumbai

27.

29 September 1999. Jennifer née Pinky Francis, née Marie Hancox and now Anne Edgells turned eighteen.

However, Jennifer remembers nothing of her eighteenth birthday. 'I know I was hustling those days. It was nothing extraordinary I did that day. It was like any ordinary day. Even that I don't remember. I guess too much of weed makes you forget. Moral is, don't smoke too much of weed!' She laughs.

At eighteen Jennifer was discharged from the foster care system with no family and no one to take care of her. While most American children want to leave the family home and live independently, Jennifer was longing to be a part of a family, having lived most of her childhood years away from a home and family, and mostly on the run.

She was given $475 and food stamps to live off by the State but she had no idea how to take care of herself. She soon became homeless and started sleeping at bus stations. At some point she tried to go back to Aunt Rathe's house, who took her in for some time despite all the bad blood that flowed between them in the past. But, this arrangement did not last for long. At one point, Jennifer even tried going back to school but since her records could not be located, it marked the end of her plan to complete her education. At every point in her life it was circumstances and situations, which ruled her life rather than rationale.

It was at Aunt Rathe's, when she started seeing an African American guy called Fred who lived with his mother. She would often go to his place when she needed to feel she belonged to a family. Fred was a good-natured boy and they started dating steadily.

By now, her cousins Jess and Jen were working and Rathe put pressure on Jennifer to find a job. The erratic shoplifting and hustling was not enough for her to get by. Around this time she befriended a Chantell, a crackhead girl who had a small boy from a man called Caesar.

A Baby Daddy is a common concept in the US, when a man may not be married to the mother of his child, but takes full responsibilities towards the child like a regular 'daddy'. One example is of rapper, Kanye West, who was Kim Kardashian's Baby Daddy, till the couple tied the knot. Then, he became her husband.

Chantell promised her that Caesar would give Jennifer a job if she came to her mother's house the next day to meet up with him. Like Chantell, her mom, Malika was also a crackhead. As Jennifer stopped by at Chantell's the next day, she saw a large, young, good-looking African American man sprawled on a couch in the front porch. With a well-cut beard in a brown tee and ripped blue jeans, the handsome man seemed to be sleeping. Jennifer was hesitant to wake him and decided to call her friend. Meanwhile, Chantell came out and on seeing Jennifer led her upstairs to her room.

'Isn't Caesar sleeping outside? I didn't wanna wake him. He's sleeping like a baby,' Jennifer said.

'Oh no honey. That's not Caesar. Caesar's upstairs. That's Justin. Caesar's friend,' Chantell informed as she took Jennifer upstairs.

'Oops! Thank God I didn't wake up the wrong guy. He would've barked at me then,' Jennifer smiled.

※

'Hi there. How are you?' the handsome young man called out to Jennifer who was making her way out of Chantell's house after meeting Caesar. He was awake.

'Hi,' Jennifer smiled back.

'Hey,' the young man walked up to her, 'I'm Justin,' as he extended his hands to shake hers.

'Hi. I'm Jennifer,' she replied, flattered

'A friend of Chantell's?' Justin asked.

'Yup,' Jennifer nodded.

'Hmm. So, Jen do you have a boyfriend?'

Jennifer was taken aback by his sudden brashness and thought it rather rude, 'None of your business, dude,' she said. Justin laughed. He had a husky, full-throated laugh, which Jennifer found sexy, despite his rudeness to her.

'Okay. Okay. No need to get upset. I just asked your name. I didn't ask for your number,' Justin grinned.

'Try asking?' Jennifer challenged.

'Alright then…what's your number, babe?' Justin asked grinning.

'96806…39,' Jennifer said, deliberately flipping the last two digits.

'Got it,' Justin kept grinning as Jennifer made her way out.

※

A few days later, the phone rang in Aunt Rathe's. 'For you Jenny,' Jessica who took the phone, called out to her.

'Who's it?' Jennifer asked as she came to take the call.

'Dunno. Some guy,' Jess said as she walked towards the kitchen.

'Hi,' Jennifer said into the handset.

'Hi babes. It's me,' said the voice at the other end.

'Who's me, man? Be clear,' Jennifer asked.

'Me, Justin, babes. Remember meeting at Chantell's the other day?'

'Oh! It's you, dude,' Jennifer said almost smiling when a sudden realization dawned upon her.

'Hey man, how did you get my number?' she asked surprised.

'You gave it to me, remember?' Justin said.

'Yes…but…' She could almost hear him chuckle at the other end.

'I know. You flipped the last two digits. I flipped it back,' Justin laughed.

'Oh fuck. How did you know?' Jennifer could not help laughing at his ingenuity.

'Well…I could read from your expressions…when you hesitated at the last two digits…I thought I might try my luck…'

They both laughed. Jennifer was impressed.

※

The next day as Jennifer was walking in her lane, she saw a car approaching her. She thought it was Fred waving at her, so she waved back though a little surprised at seeing Fred driving a car. As the car stopped in front of her, Fred opened the door and pulled her in. She was a bit taken aback and before she could settle in, the car sped off. She then realized it was Justin and not Fred at the wheels. 'Hey man, what's up with you?' she was stunned. 'Are you kidnapping me?'

'Yep baby. We are going for a movie,' Justin simply announced.

And that was their first date. Justin took her to see a Disney animation film, *The Lost City of Atlantis*. After that they went to a fast food chain, Hot n Spicy, which was giving a good deal on chicken burgers at 29c. Jennifer had three burgers with fries and enjoyed every bit of her dinner. Pizzas and burgers top her list of favourite foods. 'I thought Justin was a weirdo. I knew he was interested in me and that he would take me somewhere romantic or a motel room… instead he took me to a cartoon film and fed me burgers and fries,' she laughs as she recollects her first date with him.

What impressed Jennifer about Justin was not his looks, but his car. 'It was the first time I dated someone with a car. He had a Chevvy,' says Jennifer. 'He used to spend a lot on his cars as he loved attracting girls with his car and the oversized sunglasses he wore.'

He was nice looking though he did not have much of an ass but a cute smile. He didn't talk much either but he gave me good vibes though initially I was not attracted to him in a sexual way as I was still dating Fred.'

Two days later there was a fight between Justin and Chantell and her crackhead mom, Malika, who broke Justin's car. The police were called in and Justin drove away to his cousin, Stephanie. Later he confessed to Jennifer that he was 'f**king both Chantell and her mom' though he was only getting a 'head' (i.e. a blow job) from them by supplying them with crack worth $20 daily as he was hustling from their house. This upset Jennifer and she 'cooled off' from Justin.

Meanwhile at Aunt Rathe's, things were getting a bit difficult as Jennifer refused to work and this compounded with her moody and difficult behaviour, led Karen to finally throw her out. She moved in with Fred but within a few days' time his mom started acting difficult with her. One afternoon, a down and out Jennifer was walking down the street from her house when Justin zoomed in in his Chevvy and 'kidnapped' her for the second time. This time he took her to a garden, somewhere between Battle Creek and Marshall, and finally confessed to being in love with Jennifer. He sealed his declaration with a passionate kiss to which Jennifer responded fervently. When he found out her predicament he immediately gave her $200 and bought her steaks from a grocery store. They then went to Fred's and made the steaks and had them for dinner. Fred and his mother were not home at the time.

Though Jennifer responded to Justin's passionate kissing, she was still not sure whether to pursue Justin as she was still in a relationship with Fred. The next day Justin drove down to Fred's, parking his Chevvy a little ahead of the house and asked Jennifer to join him in Chicago. She was not sure and Justin threatened to kidnap her if she refused. Jennifer was scared and ran away. Later Fred's mother brought her back home. A few days later he asked her again to go with him to Chicago or else threatened to kidnap her. Jennifer was very confused—whether to leave Fred and go with Justin into the unknown or stay in familiar surroundings in an unsteady relationship with Fred. Justin left his mobile phone with her and gave her three days to decide whether she wanted to be with him or not. When Fred saw the mobile phone, he was seething with anger and beat her with his ring that gave her a black eye. At that moment she decided she wanted to be with Justin as she 'did not want to be in an abusive relationship' for the rest of her life.

When Justin returned three days later, Jennifer had made up her mind. She decided to move on in life and move in with Justin.

※

The next day Jennifer left a note for Fred and his mother saying that she was moving out and 'don't come looking for me dude'. She left with Justin, who took her to Motel 6 in Battle Creek and they checked in as a couple. As they entered the neat little room, Jennifer went to one side of the bed and slept like a baby. When she woke up, she noticed Justin smiling at her while he flipped channels on the TV on the other side of the bed. 'What about some grub babe? Been hungry. Waiting for you to surface from la la land,' Justin asked.

'Yeah, why not. Am famished.'

Justin took her to Wendy's nearby and then to the local Sear's and bought her a few clothes. Jennifer saw Justin pull out the bills from his bill-fold with ease as he paid for the items. But it was difficult to rid herself of old habits, and so Jennifer managed to slip in a tee and a pair of slacks under her clothing. But Justin did not get to know of this, as it was safely tucked underneath her clothes, tag and all.

Once in the room and they had changed for the night, Justin held Jennifer and gave her a smouldering kiss. Jennifer responded. She then released herself from Justin's embrace and went to her side of the bed and sat. 'Sorry dude...I mean no offence. You know I like you enough to move in with you...but I need some time. I hope you understand. I'm just out of a relationship and you are a stranger... just give me some time dude.'

'Take all the time in the world honey. I am in no hurry. We have all the time,' Justin said.

For the next few days they stayed on in Motel 6, moving around during the day and getting to know each other and sharing the same bed at night in a platonic manner. 'I felt safe and comfortable with him,' Jennifer reminisces. 'Any other guy would just wanna jam the thing inside and then cut me off.'

On the third day, Justin drove to a small apartment block and asked Jennifer to deliver a packet wrapped in a newspaper to 'the blonde-dyed black chick called Celia in apartment 402'. 'And come back soon,' Justin advised. Jennifer nodded. Jennifer did as she was told while Justin waited in the car. Celia on seeing Jennifer quickly ran in to the house and came back with a stash of dollars. Taking the packet from Jennifer, she gave her the cash. Jennifer refused and went down. Seeing her, Justin asked, 'Where's the money?'

'What money?'

'Didn't Celia give you no money?' Justin asked. Jennifer nodded hesitatingly. 'Then where's it?'

'I didn't take no money from her though she was giving me some.'

'But why?'

'Coz you never mentioned any money thing dude…'

Justin put up his hands in exasperation at Jennifer's reply. 'Alright. My fault. I should've warned you. Now run up and ask Celia for the money. I'll also call her from my mobile,' Justin said as Jennifer headed back to the apartment.

The next day Jennifer and Justin were sitting at Dennis, a twenty-four-hour diner over a late lunch when Jennifer probed Justin. 'Now that I am planning to move in with you and will soon be committing myself to you, I just wanted to know what do you do?' Jennifer asked.

'Huh?' Justin looked up with his mouth full of cheesy fries.

'I mean what work do you do? What is your line of business?'

'Ah. I work with Jesse.' Jesse Cobbs was Justin's stepfather, whom his mother Judy had married.

'And what is his line of business?'

'Construction.' Justin replied still busy negotiating the cheesy fries.

'And what exactly do you do in construction?' Jennifer persisted.

'This n that…' Justin shrugged.

'What exactly do you do Justin?' Jennifer was firm.

'Whaddya mean?' Justin looked at her, wiping the cheese from his mouth.

'Look you be honest with me dude. Or else I ain't going with you nowhere.' Jennifer almost got up to go.

'Relax babe. Chill.' Then after a pregnant pause, Justin said, 'Alright. I'm hustling. I'm selling crack.'

Jennifer looked at him unsurprised as Justin continued.

'I've been selling crack for as long as I can remember. In fact, most of my family members apart from Judy, deal in drugs. Mainly cocaine. Especially crack. We've been in the business for three generations now…' Justin broke off chuckling. 'Although I sell crack, I never do crack. Never done it. Swear to you. I've only done weed, mushroom and ecstasy.'

'So that's that. But I'm not tellin' you where I get my stuff. Now that I've come clean, are you with me or not?'

Jennifer pondered for a bit. There was nothing much happening in her life right now. She had no job, no family and no place to stay. Fred and she were through. There was no savings and she had no clue what she would be doing in the future for a living. She was living life on the edge. Justin, despite his dealing in crack, seemed a far steadier and safer option than her current situation. Jennifer looked up at Justin who was watching her. She smiled at him.

'Fuck it. I'm with you dude.'

And so began a new chapter in Jennifer Francis Hancox Edgell's life.

28.

After her decision to go along with Justin, Jennifer felt a sense of security and belonging. However, Justin had to immediately go out on an important assignment and asked Jennifer to hang around in Battle Creek until his return. They checked out of Motel 6. Going back to Fred's was impossible, especially after the 'stinker missile' she left before leaving his house. She did not want to crash at Chantell's either because of Justin's association with them. Finally, the only place left to move in was at Aunt Rathe's. Jennifer begged her aunt to let her stay for a few days before she left for Chicago, 'lock, stock 'n' a smoking barrel'. Rathe agreed.

Before leaving, Justin had given her two shoeboxes and told her to keep them carefully. One was stashed with greenbacks and the other with crack cocaine. Jennifer was sharing the room with Leah, her youngest cousin, who knew about the 'shoeboxes'. The Rathes only ate together but led separate lives. Jennifer was protective about Leah, who was a pretty sixteen year old. She did not approve of her boyfriend who dealt in weed and therefore she kept telling Leah to 'stay off him'. Leah obviously did not relent. One day over an argument, Jennifer told Aunt Rathe on Leah. 'Karen busted Leah's ass and Leah busted my ass by telling on the two shoeboxes,' says Jennifer. Karen Rathe finally threw Jennifer out of her house for good as she 'wanted nothing to do with drugs'.

It was only after Jennifer was thrown out that Justin and she seriously started living together. What endeared Justin most to Jennifer was that she had a sort of fearlessness about her. Back then Justin considered himself weak, but he got strength from Jennifer.

'I don't know when I fell in love with Jennifer, but I love her and still do. Probably will always love her. No matter what happens between us, she will FOREVER be my friend and I will do anything for her. And even take a bullet for her,' writes Justin Ashley Haynes, after all these years from the Federal Correction Centre (Unit B) in Sandstone, Michigan.

※

At this time, Jennifer moved in with Stephanie, Justin's first cousin, who stayed in Battle Creek. Stephanie worked as a nurse but her mother, Margaret Grace, who was also Judy's sister, was 'dealing and doing cocaine'. 'She was not a crackhead though,' admits Jennifer though she did cocaine. 'She worked and lived with her boyfriend in Echo Street.'

Justin, who mainly got his supplies from Chicago, now went into business with Grace. Justin would get his supplies on credit from Chicago to sell in and around Battle Creek. The two were now doing business from Ramada Inn. One day Jennifer overheard Justin and Grace arguing on the phone. Grace wanted a higher percentage from Justin, which he refused as he felt he was already paying her well. One night they had just retired when there was a knock on their room door. Justin had taken off his contact lenses so asked Jennifer to answer the door and deal with the customers, if any. As she opened the door, she saw it was Grace's stepson with two guys, who appeared like goons. Grace had hired the two goons, who robbed them of all their cocaine and money. The police came in and they were thrown out of the hotel and had to move into a small motel on the outskirts of the city.

Justin was devastated at being betrayed by his own aunt and also for the huge loss he had incurred. He had to pay his creditors as well. He mustered up the courage to call his mother and told her everything. Judy, though vehemently against his drug dealings, called her son over, knowing he was going through a rough patch.

'Battle Creek is no good for me Jenny. I'll have to go back to Chicago. My folks are there. My pals are there. You wanna come with me?' he asked. 'But feel free to say no. I will not mind. But I cannot stay on here anymore,' said Justin.

Having nowhere else to go in Battle Creek, Jennifer made up her mind.

'Am with you dude. I'll go to Chicago with you.'

❦

29.

Chicago.

This Midwestern Illinoisan city is the third-most populous city in the US with over three million residents. It is the world's seventh-most expensive city, having the busiest airport in the globe, O'Hare International Airport. Chicago's contribution to the arts is notable especially in the field of music (jazz, soul and blues) and sports.

However, Chicago of the twentieth century is often associated with gangsters and gang warfare. The city earned this notoriety mainly due to and after the ratification of the 18th Amendment to the Constitution in 1919, which made the production, exportation and sale of alcoholic beverages in the US illegal. Between 1919 and 1933 (when the Prohibition was repealed) was what we know as the Gangster Era. This was the time when Al Capone, Dion O'Banion, Bugs Moran and Tony Accardo battled the law-enforcing agencies and each other on the streets of Chicago to establish their supremacy over the illegal trade.

Gangs in the US today include several types of groups, national street gangs, local street gangs, prison gangs, motorcycle gangs, ethnic and organized crime gangs. Most of these gangs operate in urban areas such as Los Angeles, Miami, Philadelphia, New York and of course Chicago. The reasons for becoming members of these gangs are varied: profiting from organized crime to protection from rival gangs to family tradition, or simply for the sake of personal status and being 'cool'.

From gambling to drug and arms trafficking to counterfeiting to human trafficking and prostitution, there is a wide range of activities covered by gangs today. Prison gangs are formed mainly to protect from rival gangs. For many gangsters, reaching the 'prison gang status' is the ultimate commitment to a gang.

During the 1990s, the southern parts of America saw an increase in gang activity, and it is believed that two per cent of the US military was affiliated with a gang. It also noted the introduction of crack cocaine that was used to purchase unprecedented amounts of weaponry.

Four Corner Hustlers started out as a single gang, which was started in 1969 by Walter Wheat and Freddy Malik Gauge. All the gang members wore black or black and red or black and gold, and their main dealing was drugs in Chicago and Kansas City.

Justin Ashley Haynes was a member of the Four Corner Hustlers.

Since Justin was hustling quite a bit in those days, it was but wise for him to have the support of a gang. One day some members of the gang based in Chicago's Maywood district, beat up Justin. Justin didn't say a word and took it all in. He was then inducted as a member. The bashing up was an initiation into the gang. It was then that Judy decided to send him to Battle Creek.

When Jennifer arrived in Chicago with Justin, she was as nervous about meeting Justin's mom, Judy. But, she was mesmerized by the city. Judy stayed in a very stylish area of Chicago called Rutherford in Oak Park, about twenty minutes from downtown, with her husband, Jesse Cobbs, Justin's stepfather. Judy was in a relationship with Justin's father, though they were not married. They lived in a pretty house that was 'very stylish and posh like the lady herself', admits Jennifer.

Judy Cobbs, née Robertson, née Ansley grew up in Battle Creek. Coincidently, Blaine Edgell and Judy Ansley went to the same school though Judy recollects nothing about Blaine. Judy grew up in a large family of ten brothers and sisters, Maurice, Dave, Reuben, Memen,

Grace, Thelma and Beth along with her mother and stepfather. The family had been dealing in drugs for the past two generations and several members, especially Grace, had served jail terms for hustling. After graduating from high school, she moved to Chicago and went to college and gradually distanced herself from her drug-dealing family. 'All was not happy there, but I had fun as a kid, loved school and played the flute,' is how Judy likes to sum up her childhood.

With a degree in business administration from the prestigious Elmhurst College, Judy worked with the well-known law firm, Seigal as an accounts manager and lived lavishly unlike her African American family.

Judy was first married to a Mr Robertson but soon split up. She then met and lived with Wayne Haynes, Justin's father, whom she had met when she was fourteen on a visit to Chicago. Wayne was a truck driver and would blow up all his salary on drugs and alcohol and pick up prostitutes and spent most of his time in bars. But, during the time he wooed Judy, he would drive all the way from Chicago to Battle Creek in his old Cadillac, wearing gold chains and impress her with his hustling money. However, soon after Justin's birth, things between the two deteriorated because of Wayne's womanizing ways and Judy moved out of his life.

Judy struggled to bring up Justin while working full time, leaving the child alone at home mostly. 'Wayne took no financial responsibility and I didn't have a lot of money. I had to struggle to make ends meet. That was not fun,' says Judy, adding, 'Wayne was a lousy father though his father Willie did keep the boy for a couple of years.'

Justin of course did not have his mother's penchant for studies, and instead loved the good things in life. 'He had a difficult time in school because he had behavioural problems there as well as with me though I sent him to one of the best schools in the district, Oak Park. He did not graduate from high school. He ended up getting a GED or the state's general equivalency exams to pass,' says Judy.

'He started hustling from a young age. Fourteen to be precise,' recollects Judy. When she first found out about Justin's association with drugs, she was 'sad, extremely sad. I talked about it to those who would listen. I also went to see a therapist. Eventually Justin moved to another state.'

Later Judy married Jesse Cobbs, who though was good to her, never took to Justin. Neither was Jesse a good father to his biological children from his previous marriage.

Jennifer sums Judy up best. 'She is a Black who thinks like a White.'

※

On reaching Chicago, the couple headed straight to Judy's place. Judy welcomed Jennifer warmly with a tight hug. Over a glass of wine and the Chinese meal she had ordered, Judy chatted with Jennifer while Jesse and Justin barely spoke.

'So Justin my boy how many more girlfriends are you going to bring home?' Justin looked embarrassed and Jennifer looked worried but Judy explained, 'I'm joking honey. You are the second girl he has brought home.' Then turning to her son she said, 'I hope you will be serious this time.'

By the end of the evening, Jennifer was totally in love with Judy Cobbs. 'I am stealing your mom,' she told Justin.

'Glad you girls like each other,' Justin replied.

The evening ended with Judy gifting Jennifer a basket of bath and beauty products from Bath & Beyond, the most stylish gift Jennifer had received from anyone.

Judy's first impression of Jennifer then was, 'A good girl, who needed a family who could love her.'

※

In Chicago it was not easy-going for Justin and Jennifer. They did not stay with Judy since Jesse did not want them home. So the next obvious place for them to stay was at shelter homes. These shelters were mostly within church precincts meant for the poor and homeless. The process was this: You go to a church that has a shelter and stand in queue; if the beds are free then you get to sleep there that night. However, during the day you will have to vacate the place and find a public bath to bathe and clean. Justin and Jennifer went to Judy's to bathe and eat, as Jesse just about tolerated their presence during those few hours in the house.

Jennifer hated her nights in Chicago and having to sleep in shelters. It humiliated her to no end, but Justin assured her that it was only a matter of time and things would soon improve. However, Jennifer was not easily pacified and cried a lot. She especially freaked out when on her first night at a shelter she saw a man having a seizure.

Around this time Justin and Jennifer would also use the premises of one of Judy's aunts—an old lady called Annie Cole, who lived by herself and also hustled—to bathe and change. Annie Cole hated girls so Jennifer had to dress like a boy to hoodwink her into letting her in her house and use her bathroom. One day while the couple were bathing, the old lady yelled, 'I can hear a girl's voice.' Henceforth they bathed quietly.

One day Annie Cole gave a cheque of $2,000 to Justin to cash it for her. Since they were hard of cash, Justin gave it to Jennifer to encash it and they never returned to Annie Cole's. Later, both felt bad for robbing her. They wanted to return her money and in order to return the $2,000, they decided to rob a bank! Justin and Jennifer decided to research on the subject at the local library.

Since people had to leave the shelter by six in the morning, the duo spent their mornings from 6 a.m. to 8 a.m. in a public garden. When the local public library in Oak Park, near Judy's house opened, both of them trooped in and spent hours reading books on how to rob a bank! If only they had spent the same energy and effort to work towards a decent living! But, the idea was to 'get rich quick and easy', little realizing that quick-fix ways also wear out quickly.

Amongst the tips given in the book to conduct a bank robbery was to slip a note to the cashier with the writing 'Please just give me all the cash without making a noise or I'll fix you.' According to the book, this method worked better than a gun. This suited them fine since they did not have the money to invest in a gun. They targeted a small bank in the area near the Plaza. Everything was planned. Just before entering the bank they decided they would distract the police and while the police's attention was elsewhere, they would do their job and get away with the loot. Easy. But easier said than done.

On the morning of the robbery, Justin made a hoax call to the police telling them there was a bomb at the other end of the Plaza, away from the bank. Unfortunately for them, the police didn't take Justin seriously and decided it was a crank call. Their plan failed miserably.

Since they were really short of money and had failed at their attempt of robbing a bank, Justin decided to return to Battle Creek and start hustling all over again.

30.

The situation for the duo was not as bright as the time they left for Chicago. Justin was doing well then, hustling and driving a Chevrolet. Now he was in debt and almost a pauper. He had to begin all over again. But, this time round he had a steady girlfriend who was also his partner in crime, Jennifer.

Justin could not afford to stay in Ramada Inn or any cheap motel, so they rented a small place, an apology for an apartment at $350 a month at 95, Battle Creek Avenue. 'It was a bogus area, full of crackheads,' Jennifer recollects. 'We were pretty much unhappy there and fought constantly over small things. We swore at each other a lot and Justin spent a night in jail for physically abusing me after I complained to the police.'

'The kitchen was full of rats and I hated cooking in there. We mostly ate out at fast food joints. There was one filthy couch and a television. We didn't last there for more than a month after which we left but not before I got termites in my body! I was in hospital for two days to treat my skin infection. It was lousy.'

❦

Their next abode was a much cleaner apartment in a nicer neighbourhood. They stayed there for a year but fought constantly. According to Jennifer, she constantly suspected Justin of cheating on her. 'He wanted me to be at home and attend to his whims while he drove around town attracting chicks. Justin liked to fancy up his cars and wore oversized glares to attract chicks. I would get pissed and from time to time steal his cocaine and money and run away. But not for long. Sooner or later I would finish the booty and get stranded. Then I would have to call him to come and pick me up,' laughs Jennifer.

Another point that brought in the fights between the couple was Justin's over generous nature and his gullibility. 'Justin never said no to anyone. However much of a mess he was in, he would still help others. He was not selfish like me. There were times he would get a lot of friends from Chicago to Battle Creek to hustle though he knew they would be poaching his clients. He would break his neck to help a homeless person. I would tell him to sort ourselves first and then do charity. But he would hear none of it. And that became a point of argument in many of our quarrels, which would often turn violent and ugly.'

'Justin loved to show off. Apart from cars and sunglasses to attract girls, he would often show off his cooking skills. One day he made a pie, a Peach Cobbler. He put it in the oven. While it was baking, we fought over something. I got pissed and went and added far too generous amounts of seasoning salt to it. When he started eating it, he choked on it and threw a piece of the pie at me. We ended up throwing Peach Cobbler at each other. He was so mad that he left and went to a strip joint. When he got back, I was so upset that I hit him hard on the butt with his rifle. Till date he has a scar on his butt,' giggles Jennifer recollecting those childish fights.

Jennifer was now assisting Justin full time in hustling. Once they had gone to deliver some 'stuff' when they were stopped by the police and questioned on a tip off. 'I had one pocket of my jeans full of weed and the other stuffed with crack. I could have easily got 30 years. So I quickly threw it discreetly outside the car...Justin was upset and we fought over it. But we saved our asses because when the police ran my name, they found out about the warrant issued in my name in Jackson,' laughs Jennifer.

Another time Jennifer was caught by the police while they were driving to Chicago. A crack pipe belonging to a crackhead, which was in the car, fell on Jennifer's side and the cops saw it. The licence and the owner of the car's name did not match. Besides, the cops found out that Justin was wanted in Battle Creek for misdemeanour. He was put in Ben Harbour Jail for a month from where he wrote Jennifer a letter apologizing and asked her to wait for him till he was back. Along with it he enclosed a cheque of twenty-five dollars.

Jennifer hovered between his cousin Stephanie's and the Salvation Army till Justin returned. Both started hustling again and slowly their fortunes turned for the better. They rented a very nice apartment in Fairland, a very posh area in the city and all seemed to be happy again. Justin taught her to drive. He cooked for her. Justin hardly visited strip joints then. He also hung around less with his druggie pals though he himself was doing WET, i.e., weed mixed in balmy fluid. 'It was very, very strong,' says Jennifer.

During this time, Justin once took very ill. He came down with a very high fever and was delirious. Jennifer nourished him back to health, staying by his bedside and cooking nourishing food for him.

As Justin was recovering, he told Jennifer:

'Jenny, I am going to ask you something.'

'What?' she asked.

'For a favour honey.'

'Now what? What favour you want from me man?'

Justin hesitated for a few seconds, then he popped the question, 'Will you marry me Jenny?'

For a moment Jennifer thought she misheard him. She had wanted to marry Justin for some time now but whenever she broached the subject with him, he avoided it or they fought over it. And now what she was hearing was too good to be true. She could not believe her ears.

'You seriously mean it man! You not pulling a fast one on me?'

'I am serious. Honest to God.'

'Oh cool! Yes dude, I wanna be married to you,' Jennifer said and kissed him passionately.

❦

Months went by since Justin proposed but there were no signs of marriage. One day while sitting on the bed in the Fairland apartment, as Justin watched TV, Jennifer said, 'Hey dude, let's get married.'

Justin replied, 'Okay.'

They set up a date, 2 July, and decided to go about applying for the licence before that. When Justin called up Judy and told her about his decision, Judy did not approve. 'Judy loved me a lot but did not approve because she thought this kind of wayward life, hustling, would not be good to raise a family. Judy belonged to Jehovah's Witness,' says Jennifer.

But nevertheless, she did attend their wedding, along with Justin's granddad, Willie Haynes. They drove down all the way from Chicago.

It was a court wedding in Battle Creek on a bright day. Jennifer wore a dark blue dress and Justin wore a red shirt and blue jeans. Rings were exchanged, a gold wedding band with a diamond combined. 'I felt very different, very flustered as the wedding vows were being exchanged,' says Jennifer.

The only other person present at their court marriage, apart from Judy and Willie was Justin's cousin, Edward. The small group trouped into Chillies for a dinner of steaks and burgers.

31.

Justin did not want to spend too much at the wedding. Instead, he decided to take Jennifer on a honeymoon; perhaps, the first holiday she had in her life. The following day they drove down to Dale in Wisconsin, which was a huge water park. On the first day of their honeymoon, they just smoked a lot of weed and slept. For the nineteen-year-old bride and the twenty-year-old groom, this could have been a fun destination to spend their honeymoon. However, things turned out differently. According to Jennifer, Justin was making a lot of money those days hustling and he would 'keep eyeing chicks'. They were in turn attracted to his money. Most of the honeymoon days, Justin spent at nightclubs. According to Justin, Jennifer quarrelled with him a lot as she 'did not know how to behave like a married woman'.

Once the honeymoon was over, the couple returned to Battle Creek. Justin started visiting strip clubs again. It was as if this habit of picking up women from strip joints and doping was a legacy passed down by Wayne to his son. Overnight, Justin became a chauvinist husband, expecting Jennifer to stay at home and do the housework while he worked out and hung around with different girls. He started moving around with a Mexican girl named Breeanna.

Jennifer questioned Justin about his affair with Bree but he flatly denied it. But her anger and jealousy worsened when she found out that instead of taking her out to hustle with him, he took Bree. She was wild when she found out that of the three cars he owned, he had put one in Bree's name. He also blocked her credit and gas cards so that she could not travel or leave the house. Though the apartment was nice and it was a posh neighbourhood, Jennifer hated staying at home all day. She developed a Lady Macbeth phobia, that of scrubbing the carpets in the house over and over again.

Despite Justin's philandering ways, she still loved him enough to want to have his child. She prayed fervently that she would be able to bear children, though she gravely doubted it. After being sexually abused as a child by Blaine Edgell in Battle Creek, she was told that her uterus had been cleaned up and she would most likely never be able to bear a child. In other words, she was rendered barren due to sexual abuse. This had bothered Jennifer on and off, but more so now as she was married and desperately wanted to have a baby. She also believed that this would be a way to keep Justin tethered to her.

As Jennifer sums up those days, 'It was after marriage our relation went downhill.'

Though Jennifer does not remember celebrating her eighteenth birthday, she remembers Justin celebrating her twenty-first birthday. Despite their uneasy relations, he took her for a Snoopdog concert—her favourite—followed by dinner and then to a very posh lounge bar. 'Though he was cheating on me with Bree, he was very nice to me that day. He also bought a car, a Chevvy and put it on my name. But he put no gas in it and blocked my credit cards, fearing I might run away. He knew my nature best.'

'During the concert Bree kept on calling him. I could see Justin torn between Bree and me. I got a feeling that day that Bree really loved him. My heart was broken when I realized this. I had no idea what to do. I was very very sad.' Jennifer recollects painfully.

Unable to drive despite having a car as all her credit cards were blocked, unable to bear being at home all day and unable to have a child, Jennifer decided to run away from it all. She was sinking into depression. She stole over five thousand dollars from Justin one day and disappeared, leaving a note for Justin not to come looking for her. She went to Marshall and stayed with a crackhead girlfriend of hers for some time, working at a Taco Bell and R&B joint. Justin would sometimes come and pick her up and take her home. They would be together for a few weeks and then she would disappear again with some cash. This went on for a year till one day Jennifer decided she had had enough.

She got in touch with her stepsister, Fatiha, who was then working as a stripper in St Louis in Missouri. Fatiha had a sugar daddy and a son Talique from him, out of wedlock. Jennifer arrived by Amtrack, very distraught and upset. She was sick and had vomited throughout the journey. Fatiha gave her half a tablet of Ecstasy and told her to take it easy. She reassured her that all would be well. Jennifer slept like a log.

The next day Fatiha took her sister to a doctor and after examining her, the doctor pronounced that Jennifer was pregnant.

Jennifer was over the moon with happiness despite the undulating turns of her married life. On her wedding day, Jennifer had quietly prayed, 'I know it is difficult, but let me see one child. That is all I ask.' It was as if God answered her prayers.

This was indeed a miracle.

She decided to return to Chicago and give Justin the good news.

Running short of money, she decided to take a bus to Chicago from Florida. It took four days and she had to change five buses. 'It was one scary experience.'

Justin was surprised to see Jennifer appear so soon and so suddenly after taking his money and fleeing. He was wondering why she looked happy and cheerful. He was very angry with her. He snapped, 'Why are you back? What do you want now?'

'Hey dude, I got news for you man. You gonna become a daddy soon. I am pregnant. Five weeks gone. I came back to give you the news. We are gonna be parents soon,' Jennifer ran up and hugged her husband. Justin tried to disentangle himself from her arms. 'Bullshit!' was all she heard him say.

'Whaddya mean? I swear, it's true, I'm gonna have a baby. God has answered my prayers. He is giving us a little baby.'

'I don't care what but I am no part of this bullshit baby. It's not my baby and I don't want to have anything to do with it,' Justin thundered.

'Hey man. Wait a minute. Whaddya mean it's not your baby?'

'You've been away for almost a year. You come and go as it pleases you. Most of the time you been on your own…so where do I figure in this baby shit? Your baby. You keep it. I ain't taking no responsibility for this baby.'

'Okay. As you wish you motherf***er. I am keeping this baby. I will raise it on my own. Though I swear to God I have been true to you you motherf***ing crackhead b*st**d,' Jennifer said with tears welling up in her eyes. Justin looked away. He was angry and sad at the same time.

It was a difficult pregnancy for Jennifer. Apart from her emotional turmoil with Justin, she also developed diabetes during the last months of her pregnancy due to excess consumption of junk food like doughnuts, bagel steaks and chicken burgers. One evening when her water broke, Justin was high and busy playing video games. He called 911 and told them to take Jennifer to the hospital. 'This motherf*** actually fell asleep while I was going into labour,' says Jennifer.

Kadafi, named after the rapper, was born on the 3 June 2004.

Jennifer was 21 and Justin 22 years. Justin kept repeating it was not his baby till Judy arrived and gave him a few resounding slaps after showing him his baby photographs. Justin noticed the similarity and slowly started to accept the boy. Kadafi was a very small and thin baby and Judy spent a few days helping Jennifer nurse Kadafi. 'Justin was jealous because all our attention was on Kadafi. He wanted to have sex all the time. I told him off.'

Two weeks after Kadafi was born Justin got busted for selling crack cocaine to an undercover agent. He got four months without a collateral.

Two months later Jennifer was pregnant for the second time. Kassana was born on 8 July 2005.

32.

While Jennifer was pregnant with Kassana, she was caught smuggling heroin in her body through Amtrack to Michigan. It was felony for possession of more than the prescribed level of 20 gm of heroin. She was put overnight in jail till Justin bailed her out the next day. But she had to serve probation for two years. Soon after, Justin was caught with heroin sometime in 2004 and was put in Newberry Prison in Michigan. It was a tough time and Jennifer was so upset that she started smoking weed despite being pregnant. In fact just before her delivery, when her water burst, she was high on weed though the doctors were clueless. Justin was out on bail for a few days when Kassana was born. Four days after Kassana was born Justin's trial for possession of heroin was on and he lost the case. He was pronounced guilty and given four-and-a-half years' sentence.

❧

It was a tough time for the family. Jennifer was left with two toddlers with no job and no savings. Jennifer was also being closely watched by the police as they suspected Justin of having secretly stashed up his heroin and crack with her. Judy came in intermittently to help out with the children but she had to go back to Chicago as she had a job to attend. She also helped out with money now and then. Jennifer stayed on in Battle Creek. She hustled now and then and drove rental cars at $25 an hour. She would visit Justin in Newberry State prison. Justin was okay with Kassana but still harboured doubts about Kadafi's paternity.

Judy warned Jennifer not to hustle at all and that it would not help if she got caught. There would be no one to look after the children. On one of her visits to Battle Creek, she collected all the remaining drugs that were stashed away and flushed it down the toilet.

Now with no hustling money, their income was zero. Life was hard.

❧

Meanwhile Judy did manage to get her a job at an ice cream shop but Jennifer did not last long there. Being used to easy money and doing very little by way of hustling, putting in long hours at the ice cream shop for a pittance was not her style. She soon quit.

For some time she was on Electronic Benefit Transfer (EBT), state pension for the economically backward with children. The EBT is an ATM card that has about $450 per month and can be cashed for rent, electricity and food. But one of the clauses for being on state pension was Jennifer had to take Work First classes from 11 a.m. to 5 p.m. daily, five days a week where they teach you 'how to get a job and keep it'. Charlotte, a friend and neighbour looked after the children and was paid by the state for doing so. Sometimes, Judy also took Kadafi with her to Chicago.

However Jennifer could not sustain such a life of hard work for a pittance. She went back to hustling again. She also started seeing other men. One was an African American guy by whom she got pregnant but aborted the baby in four months. Currently, he is in prison serving life for killing a woman. 'When Judy found out I was pregnant she was magnanimous enough to adopt the child. But when she told Justin about it, he was angry and upset. I paid $500 to get an abortion,' says Jennifer. When asked about his name, she laughs and ducks the question with 'I don't remember man. It was a one-night stand.'

'Those were very hard days. I had no clue what to do. I was angry. I was pissed. Pissed with myself and everybody around me. Once my friend Angela—also a hustler like me—and I needed money. So we stood in front of Meijer's waiting to rob someone. We saw this rich bitch, very stylish in a nice friggin' Merc. We decided to mug her and rob her. She was in her sixties. Somehow I could not do it. My heart wouldn't let me. So I turned back and Angela followed,' recalls Jennifer.

But, she admits that later she did mug someone else and got jail time.

Meanwhile, she was also serving her probation period quite successfully. This was for her conviction of unlawful possession of crack cocaine in 2004. Every month she had to report to her probation officer, John Smith. She was doing good. She was 'dropping clean'.

Dropping is the term used to indicate the checking of urine for traces of drugs, especially heroin, cocaine and meth. Jennifer insists till date that she never did cocaine, heroin or meth. Only weed. But since she was boiling and touching cocaine all the time, she insists it went into her pores and would have reflected in the narcotic tests. 'So every month when I had to take a test during my probation, I would take Niacin pills to remove traces of cocaine in my system. This was followed by drinking two gallons of water. And I always dropped clean,' smiles Jennifer impishly.

However, during her last year of probation, she 'dropped dirty'. In other words, her reports showed traces of cocaine in her system. She was sent for classes to Drugs Anonymous and had to put in 4–5 hours of community service a day for two months. She was allotted to sell furniture in a warehouse. However, like always Jennifer failed as she was not cut out for hard work. It was always the easy way out for her. She was falling behind in paying her bills and things started to fall apart.

'I told John Smith that I would rather serve jail term.' He sent her to Kalamazoo, but she ran away from there after a few days as she felt 'too closed in'. Judy looked after the children. After being on the run for five days, Jennifer turned herself in.

She was sent to a jail in Ohio. The year was 2006.

33.

Jennifer served six months in Ohio jail. She was then brought to Calhoun County Jail in Battle Creek. Situated on Michigan Street in Battle Creek, it is also known as the Calhoun County Correctional Centre (C4) and it is the only jail for regular as well as immigration offenders. Why Jennifer was taken to Calhoun County still remains a mystery. Did someone suspect her of immigration violation in Ohio? Or, was it just a matter of routine? One is not sure.

When Jennifer reached C4 it was post noon and the jail shift was changing. She noticed a row of Mexicans and another row of Black people sitting. Jennifer went and sat next to the Mexicans.

'Are you Mexican?' asked a skinny beagle-eyed man to Jennifer.

'Nope. I am American. Jennifer Haynes,' she replied.

'Hi Jennifer. I am Jayjay, the Chief Immigration Officer here.'

'Hi Jayjay.'

'What I mean Jennifer is, are you originally from Mexico?'

'Nope. I am originally from India. But I am an American citizen. Been here since twenty years.'

'Then what are you doing in the immigration violation section?' Jayjay asked. 'These guys are immigration offenders, illegal immigrants, know what I mean?'

Jennifer nodded. 'I am here for probation violation if that's what you are asking?'

'Oh. I see. Then that is on the other side,' Jayjay showed her the way.

The next day the judge gave Jennifer a 90-day sentence for probation violation.

As she was being taken to her cell, she met Jayjay in the elevator.

'Hi Jennifer. Remember me? Jayjay?' He put out his hands to her.

'Yeah man. Of course I remember you. Met you yesterday. Don't have such bad memory,' Jennifer replied.

'Ah. Yes. Yes.' Jayjay hesitated.

'You wanna tell me something?' Jennifer asked

'Yes.' Jayjay nodded. 'As a matter of fact, I was going to meet you. Good I bumped into you here. It's like this. I happened to check your papers yesterday and was curious about your name.'

'What's with my name?'

'The fact that you have so many last names.'

'Uh?' Jennifer let out a grunt.

'Jennifer Anne Hancox Edgell Haynes…'

'So?' Jennifer retorted. 'They are my family names. I have been adopted by Hancox and Edgell when I was a child from India.'

'Precisely.' Jayjay cut her short. 'You are from India and you are still an Indian.'

'Hey man, stop bullshitting. I am American. A US citizen like you. I was adopted when I was seven and have been in this country since then. Adopted by pure American folks. Get it?' Jennifer was getting upset.

'First, mind your language, Miss. Second, I am aware you were adopted into an American home. But none of your adoptive parents bothered to file your papers for US citizenship. As a result you still remain an Indian,' Jayjay explained.

'Oh really. Then how come I have been here for 20 years without papers?'

'Precisely. You have lived here all these years as a permanent resident without the relevant papers. And that still does not make you an American citizen.'

'Then how come no one said anything about it so far?'

'Precisely. No one noticed it. You were lucky. Or else you would have been deported. Now I have noticed the irregularity...you better get those papers sorted or you could be deported Miss.'

'You must be joking, man,' Jennifer laughed.

'No. I am serious, Miss. Before anyone else does, I am giving you a week's time to get those papers right. Tell your folks at home to sort it out. Otherwise I am warning you Miss, you will be deported and there is nothing anyone can do to save you then.'

Jennifer was worried though she still believed it was a joke. She thought Jayjay was just trying to throw his weight around and intimidate her.

Jennifer immediately called Judy and explained the situation. Judy immediately brought the papers Janelle Edgell had filed. They realized that Janelle had only filed the papers and had not followed it up. Hence her citizenship was not finalized. Judy offered to file it with the help of Jayjay, but the latter said he would not be able to do anything about her immigration until her probation violation term was served. Only after 90 days could they look into the immigration aspect as he explained that 'US laws and immigration laws were different'.

※

After her 90-day probation violation term was over, the Immigration Department picked up Jennifer's case. It was around this time that a lady immigration officer, whose name Jennifer cannot recollect, came from Detroit and insisted on Jennifer signing some papers. She assured her it would facilitate her US citizenship. Jennifer, though not well versed in legalities, suspected the officer's motive. She refused to sign any papers without the presence of her lawyers.

It was then that both the lady officer and Jayjay coerced her to sign. 'I don't know what they had against me but I was a difficult inmate and was rude and violent with everyone in jail including the motherf**ker Jayjay. He didn't like me and was hell bent on deporting me. He made me do solitary confinement for my rude and violent behaviour.'

'Then that b**ch [the lady immigration officer], she was all screwed up and sweet talked me saying that if I signed those papers my case would go faster to the judge. I was getting tired of being pressurized and gave in and signed those papers.'

Little did Jennifer know then that by signing those papers she had actually weakened her immigration case. By signing she agreed to the aggravated felony charges. And thus any chances of getting an US citizenship even on humanitarian grounds, was now out of question.

'Between the motherf**ker Jayjay and that screwed up b**ch, they f***ed up my life big time. I wish they both rot in hell.'

※

I decided to find out Jayjay's view on this. I called up Calhoun County Jail twice on 22 February 2017, and once on 23 February 2017, leaving two voicemail messages to get back to me on my number regarding the Jennifer Haynes case. On 23 February, I left a message for him with the operator to return my call. There has been no call from him till date.

34.

While anyone would avoid being in jail, if one is in jail, they try to make the most of it. You try your best to get accustomed to it. So did Jennifer. She tried her best to acclimatize to life in jail, though she herself admits she was a difficult inmate.

Jennifer's Jail Diaries

Calhoun County was not a bad jail though the food was awful. And of course there was just one TV in the common room.

The Ohio jail was way better as there was a TV in each room and there were only two inmates per room. Even when it was overcrowded, and there were more people to accommodate, inmates sharing a room never exceeded four.

In Calhoun County there were various Pods or Sections. Each pods had several rooms. There were Pods A–Z; A–C had only women and D–Z were all men. There were a lot of women though. This was the only jail for immigration as well as regular offenders.

Each Pod had a common room that had a TV and numerous board games. There was a Visitor's Area, where you could talk to your visitor over the phone through a glass partition. Each inmate was assigned a particular day of the week to have visitors. My day was Tuesday. Judy would visit me once in a while with the children and I would be over the moon. Other than that my stepbrother Jay visited me a couple of times. I didn't have any other visitors.

However, Justin made up for this by writing to me every

other day. He was serving his four-and-a-half-year term in Newberry Prison up north in Michigan. His letters varied from love to anger to sadness. It would mainly comprise questions and answers. We sent each other questions, and we replied too.

Since this was an immigration jail as well, every Tuesday a whole lot of Mexicans would arrive and they would leave the following Tuesday as they would be sent back to Mexico. I remember one young girl was caught five times and sent back five times! They were a stubborn lot, these Mexicans.

We were woken up each morning at an unearthly 5 a.m. It was the toughest thing for me coz that used to be midnight for me. Then they used to have a roll call. After the roll call we were all served breakfast which mainly consisted of eggs, oatmeal, milk, potatoes and bread. With your own money you could order special food. It was the men who cooked.

On Thursdays I used to buy fried chicken, fries and Coke for $5. On Thursdays we could also order our toiletries, snacks and stationery from the Commissary.

After breakfast the inmates had to participate in the work programme (go out and work and return to the prison after a few hours) or prison services (kitchen, laundry, cleaning). I didn't do a work programme, but I did prison services. I would clean my room and also clean the visitation rooms. I also collected trashcans and garbage and cleaned toilets. On Fridays, me and the other women collected the laundry and would distribute it in the rooms. The washing was done by the men.

I normally bathed around 7.30 a.m. and then we could walk or exercise in a big room known as the recreation room.

Lunch was served at 11 a.m. and would be mainly hot dogs, potatoes, meats such as beef or pork, and other starchy foods. There were very little vegetables. After lunch we would be locked in our rooms till about 3 p.m., when the shift would change. I usually slept at this time. Around 4 p.m. we were allowed to walk in the jail yard and if we wanted coffee or tea we had to order it with our money. Unlike in prison, where the facilities were better, in jail we were not allowed to smoke. That was the toughest. I really missed weed. I ate and ate to cover up my craving for weed and I put on a huge amount of weight. I was so fat. I was as big as a house, man!

Dinner was served at 5 p.m. It was usually meat patty with mashed potatoes in gravy or a quiche. Food was lousy coz they wanted you to order from the Commissary. After dinner, we were locked into our rooms for about half an hour as the shift changed and then we were allowed to watch TV and play board games.

By 8.30 p.m. were sent back to our rooms and by 10.30 p.m. the lights were out. But I would keep the lights in my room on as I usually read through the night. Sometimes I ended up sleeping all day as I was awake all night. And I ended up missing out on some of my meals too.

Judy sent $25 every fortnight and Justin sent letters every two days. Once in a while, he would also send his prison cheques to me. That was sweet.

We were not allowed to discuss our offences or cases with our fellow inmates. We were also not allowed to know our local news; we were not given any news of Battle Creek in Calhoun County. We were however allowed to read the national and international news. For example, we never got *Battle Creek Enquirer*, but got *USA Today*.

Once I went into depression and didn't eat for some days. I was so constipated that I nearly killed my roommate with my farting. I don't remember most of my roomies' names. I had several and they were mainly immigration offenders. One of them seemed such a nice chick called Ruth Ann. She was jailed for killing her baby with excess cough syrup. It was hard to believe.

I couldn't adjust with a lot of inmates. I used to get

depressed and be rude. I used to fight a lot. Once I fought with a Black lady and was sent to do solitary. I was all by myself. It was scary. I did it for a fortnight and it has f**ked me up big time.

I suffered insomnia after that and had to be medicated.

Another time I was friendly with a Chinese chick, who was a prostitute by profession. I liked her. Once another inmate, Della, called her a slut and I beat the shit out of Della. I was put in solitary for a month and that completely f**ked up my brains. The other inmates were scared of me. I became quite famous, or infamous, as they say.

Our uniform was orange pyjama-shirts. Some inmates were given special responsibilities and were called trustees. They also had special privileges and wore burgundy pyjama-shirts instead of orange. I was also made a trustee once. But, I could not sustain it as my brain was completely messed up and all I was interested was to find the easy way out. I was always plotting to escape. The cameras caught me trying to escape while putting out the garbage and that ended my special privileges.

I had a whole lot of messed up roomies and inmates. There was this ugly African woman who killed her own child. Then there was this girl Brandy, who was charged for killing her grandparents for money. All this and many other incidents made me suicidal at one point. Thank God there was no fan in the cell or else I would have hung myself with the bed linen!

When Jennifer got her deportation orders, she prayed not to be deported to India. She would have preferred Calhoun County Jail to India. To her India was a strange country and the US was home and family. When her deportation orders came, she was devastated. She wanted to commit suicide again. She had no idea how to deal with the future in a foreign land.

'Every day, I feel I am trapped in a world of not my making,' is how she sums up her life with tears.

35.

On 2 July 2008, Jennifer was deported to India on a Delta Airlines flight to Mumbai.

After landing in Mumbai, Jennifer spent a month at the YMCA in Colaba and then stayed at Ashraya, a shelter home for distressed women in Chembur for more than two years.

In 2011, she got her Indian passport with great difficulty and finally became a citizen of the land of her birth again.

Soon after, she decided to move out of the shelter home and start life on her own in Mumbai after realizing that her chances of returning to the US were bleak, despite ACT and Pradeep fighting hard for her case on humanitarian grounds.

Nurturing a hope somewhere of returning to the US some day, Jennifer meanwhile decided to start life afresh in Mumbai.

Two years after Jennifer came to India, she headed out to Ghansoli to stay with her best friend from Ashraya, Rina.

Initially in Ashraya Jennifer did not get along with the quiet Rina. Rina was hard working unlike Jennifer, who lived life on the edge without a care for the future, spending most of her waking hours smoking weed. While in Ashraya, Rina attended a three-years beautician's course. After she completed her course, Sister Jane and Father Fonseca helped open a parlour for her in Ghansoli, near Thane. It was called Rina's Parlour. Jennifer used to go to the parlour daily in order to get away from the shelter home. She was not getting along with the other girls there. Between 10.30 a.m. and 6.30 p.m., Jennifer would hang around in her salon, watching films on her DVD player. Sometimes if Rina was short-staffed, Jennifer would help out. She could manage basic stuff like eyebrow threading and applying nail polish. The parlour was not doing too well and there were not too many customers.

Around this time Sister Jane was returning to her native state of Kerala. She was worried that Jennifer would not be able to get along with the other residents like Anasuya. She got into a lot of fights with them. They would ask her to drink with them and she refused. Anasuya also tried to hit on her and Jennifer rebuffed her. Anasuya was obsessed with Jennifer. Lesbianism was common in these all-girls' shelter homes. Besides this, Jennifer also did not get along with the other nuns such as Claire and Sarita. She decided to move on after Sister Jane left. She asked Rina if she could move in and share the apartment with her. They shared the five thousand rupees rent between them. Rina agreed happily as by then the two had become very close friends.

✼

Jennifer also got her first job in a US process call centre in Airoli, not too far from Ghansoli. She found out about it from a consultant in Just Dial Services. It was called Nerul IT and she was getting a salary of fifteen thousand rupees a month. She did the graveyard shift, working from 7 p.m. till 8 a.m. in the morning. Her job profile was Skip Tracing, and it entailed chasing people who owed money to banks and had disappeared without paying up. She would pretend to be from the FedEx and inform the receiver that a parcel had to be delivered. That way they would get the postal address of the debtor. Sometimes, they would trace their addresses through their relatives.

Though she had to dress more formally to office, something

Jennifer was not used to at all, having lived in jeans and tees and slippers all her life, she nevertheless tried her best. She remembers her boss Sohel Bomaywalla, a 27-year-old guy, whom she liked a lot 'though he made us slog our ass off'. Sohel was very keen to go to the US then. The year was 2012. Those were happy days.

Rina had been seeing a guy named Sunny, who did nothing much professionally. When Sunny and Rina married, he moved into the apartment with the girls. Sunny by virtue of being married to Rina, refused to share in the rent. All he did was sit at home and drink, work intermittently, spend Rina's hard-earned money and when she refused to give him money, he beat her up. Around this time, Jennifer also left Nerul IT after working there for over six months because the management had been rude to her. Besides, the timings were difficult to adjust to, she did not have enough time for herself. Also, there was no time to talk with her children.

Soon after, she joined another call centre called Leister at Tubey. This time she got a salary hike of ₹20,000. She continued with the graveyard shift, except the timings were from 6 p.m. to 6 a.m. Her job profile here was customer servicing, which mainly involved dealing with the problems of their computer servicing. Jennifer normally found out the problems and accordingly connected the clients to appropriate technicians. Despite having odd work hours and returning to a house with Rina's husband hanging around like a lazy lout, Jennifer managed to keep her job and sanity intact.

The one unfortunate incident around this time was Justin getting a life term. While Jennifer was in Ashraya, Justin was out on parole. He was doing well though he was living with a half Mexican and half White girl called Britney, with whom he has a baby girl, Kiara. He was hustling and doing well. Though Jennifer was heartbroken when she heard of his affair, she nevertheless forgave him.

But, she got the shock of her life when she got the news that Justin was caught with three kilograms of cocaine in a hotel in Battle Creek and had been taken to Calhoun County Jail. He was later convicted and got a 33-year Federal term. 'I thought he was a stupid asshole to screw up his life like this soon after parole,' says Jennifer.

She was more stressed about the children. The onus of looking after two small children fell on Judy. Initially, she continued with her full-time job as she put Kassana and Kadafi in daycare. But when the government stopped paying for the daycare, Judy quit her job and looked after the children. Currently, she works part time in a law firm.

Despite their blow-hot-blow-cold relationship and Jennifer's tendency to 'play two between the middle' according to Judy, Jennifer remains truly grateful and fond of her mother-in-law. 'She is the mom I never had, she is the friend who always stood by me, and she is the angel God sent to look after my babies. I don't know how I could manage without her,' admits Jennifer, and in the same breath saying, 'Though she can be a pain at times.'

That is Jennifer for you.

36.

What really went wrong for Jennifer legally?

Everything. Yet nothing.

Jennifer's case is one of the strangest cases in Indian legal history or in the legal history of child trafficking.

To begin with, Clarice D'Souza produced an affidavit from the Bombay High Court saying that Jennifer was abandoned by her parents and therefore free for adoption. This was perfectly legal. On this basis, a passport was issued to her without her last name, and Clarice's name appeared as her legal guardian. Again, perfectly legal, and with these two legitimate documents Jennifer left India legally as an eight year old.

In the US too her adoption papers were legally processed in both her adoptive homes. Only her citizenship papers could not as she did not stay long enough in either of her adoptive homes for her guardians to follow up on it. But then again according to the Rundles' report she had her US citizenship minus a passport.

In a way no one but the state should be responsible for this as it was the duty of the state to process her citizenship while she was under the US foster care system.

But then we cannot blame the US because according to Jennifer, she herself is responsible for this. She blames Jayjay, the Immigration Officer at Calhoun County Jail, who, under the pretext of making her accept her charges of aggravated felony, also made her sign her deportation papers and took advantage of her legal ignorance, which makes him responsible.

You can make a felon serve his jail term for felony but you cannot deport him/her to another country. In this case, even though Jennifer was not a US citizen, she was a permanent legal resident of the country. And owing to her previous circumstances, if her citizenship papers had not been processed, it was the duty of the state to have immediately sorted them out so that after serving her jail term for felony, she could walk out of prison as a free American citizen.

Although, technically Jennifer had not got her citizenship, this should not have been a reason for her merciless deportation. The system should have taken into account her two decades of residency there and her marriage to a US citizen, and automatically made her a citizen by both marriage and residency.

In a basket of apples, if one apple has a slight wart, you don't throw away the apple. You just cut out the wart and let it remain in the basket.

So why was Jennifer, an American, deported to India. Only because she was a felon?

Also, what is even more peculiar is that the Indian Embassy was in a tearing hurry to process her deportation papers to India. The then ambassador Meera Shankar did not look into Jennifer's case, which she should have on humanitarian grounds, especially since Jennifer was leaving behind two toddlers. It is possible that she did not study her case history at all. Had she done that, she would have told the US government that technically Jennifer did not belong to India at all as she was sent for adoption to the US. And since the US authorities had taken her in as an eight year old, it was therefore its duty to keep her in the US as a twenty-eight year old!

But as social worker Sangeeta Punekar says, 'We love to bow down to the White man's command.'

So perhaps, Meera Shankar was following what all Indians tend to do—follow the White man's orders.

I decided to get in touch with Meera Shankar, who has since retired from the Indian Foreign services and is currently serving on the board of Indian Tobacco Company (ITC), a huge corporate conglomerate. After having left several messages through her PA, Anjali Kukriti, and sending out two e-mails to her to get her views on this matter, she has not bothered to reply or call back.

37.

When ACT and Pradeep decided to fight Jennifer's case in the Bombay High Court to send her back to the US to her children, they were already on weak grounds legally. The damage had already been done by the Indian Embassy in Washington DC.

First and foremost, it is an impossible task for any person with a legal background to even begin to conceptualize on how to send back Jennifer. It is unlikely such relief could be granted by any court in India, since no Indian court has any domain or jurisdiction over any other country.

So, the big question remained—what could be done.

As the old saying goes, 'Where there is a law, there is a loophole', it was now for Pradeep to find the legit loophole within the law. The only way the US government could be brought to its knees vis-à-vis Jennifer, was not to hit out directly but to hit at the root of it. The organization that took her there was AIAA, the biggest adoption agency in the US. The licence to AIAA was given by the Indian government agency, CARA. Pradeep wanted AIAA's registration or licence given by CARA cancelled so that AIAA would pressurize the US government, and the US government would in turn accept Jennifer back on humanitarian grounds.

But on what basis could ACT or Pradeep ask for AIAA to be deregistered by CARA?

The only way out was to stick to the truth and show that Jennifer was in fact a 'kidnapped child' and not 'abandoned and free for adoption' as was falsely testified by Clarice in court in her affidavit on behalf of the Kuan Yin Charitable Trust in 1989. Kuan Yin was the Indian counterpart of AIAA that kidnapped and illegally trafficked Jennifer to the US, thus making AIAA an accomplice.

Clarice had also misled the court saying Jennifer was 'willingly given up by her mother' and later led Jennifer into believing that her parents were dead. However, when Jennifer located her brother Christopher and father Bosco in Ambernath, Christopher gave a testimony in court claiming Clarice D'Souza's affidavit as false.

In his affidavit filed on 20 November 2012, Christopher alias Jony Francis, son of Bosco and Wilma Francis says amongst other things that he was a child when Jennifer was sent to school by his mother. When his mother went to meet Jennifer she was told by Clarice that she was sent to the US for higher studies. Clarice also told Wilma that she had signed away her rights to her daughter. Jennifer's illegal adoption/trafficking was a sore point with their parents, Bosco and Wilma, who fought over it. Bosco also mentioned that he took to alcohol while Wilma went into depression over Jennifer's disappearance and eventually died in 2006.

Christopher further states: 'I saw my mother in sorrow and pain all her life since she understood that she lost her daughter and that the separation from her daughter was forceful. And now my sister Jennifer is also in a similar kind of situation and so I can understand her situation and feel her pain.'

❦

Pradeep filed a petition on behalf of *Jennifer Haynes Vs The Union of India and CARA* in the Bombay High Court with all the documents showing Jennifer was illegally trafficked out of India. Things started to move and CARA was putting the pressure on AIAA to have the US government take Jennifer back. Jennifer's case was making headlines and she even appeared in Arnab Goswami's show on Times Now.

Pradeep says, 'Though Justice D.Y. Chandrachud gave a favourable order in the High Court, it was only an interim order.'

The Order highlighted:

> the grave dangers that can result in the process of an inter-country adoption in the absence of due supervision and control...that despite the Union of India accepting the repatriation of the Petitioner Jennifer...she continues to be separated from her family and two minor children and living in a shelter home with no source of livelihood...the facts which have emerged before the Court even at this prima facie state is a matter of grave concern... and that it is the responsibility of the Fourth Respondent (CARA) to look into the matter within six weeks of this order as to why such as the present state of the Petitioner has come to pass...

However, when the matter came up for the final hearing and the Bench changed, the order was also reversed. CARA immediately washed its hands off Jennifer's case, saying it had nothing to do with the adoption since Jennifer was sent for adoption in 1989 while CARA was established in June 1990.

AIAA and Kuan Yin were represented by counsel Jerry Coelho, whose main source of argument was to garner sympathy for Clarice on account of her age. She was 85 years old at the time.

According to Pradeep, 'We were almost there towards our goal. Had we had sensitive judges, we would have won the case. AIAA would have had its licence cancelled. Jennifer would have been in the US now. Unfortunately, except for Justice Chandrachud's interim order, which was in favour of looking at Jennifer's case in a humanitarian manner, the others did not.'

The final Order from the Bombay High Court on 12 April 2010, with Justice Mridula Bhatkar on the Bench spelt:

> ...the inter-country adoption at the relevant time did not include obtaining a citizenship of the said country, though it does now....in the given facts and circumstances it would have been wiser for the Respondents (AIAA and Kuan Yin) to bring this to the notice of the Court but they cannot be blamed for this non action disproportionately as they kept the Petitioner (Jennifer) in foster care system...therefore we are not inclined to entertain a prayer for cancelling the registration of Respondent No. 2 (AIAA)...'

ACT and Pradeep decided to take the matter to the Supreme Court of India. For some time, the Supreme Court was also very sympathetic to Jennifer's case. One judge, Justice Gyan Sudha Misra was especially understanding, and keen on granting permission to de-license AIAA. 'But then the Bench changed and not everyone is as sensitive to the matter as their predecessor. Hence our appeal was rejected in the highest court of the country,' says Pradeep. He goes on to add, 'Much later Justice Misra wanted to reopen Jennifer's case vis-à-vis another matter which was similar in nature. She wanted to revise on the final Supreme Court order. Unfortunately by the time the matter came up, she had retired.'

Justice Misra herself recollects the Jennifer Haynes' case after all these years. 'Yes I remember it clearly. And I totally empathized with Jennifer. It was not her fault and she needed to go back to her minor children. And this could be achieved but it needed government intervention from the highest sources. Since I am passionate about this cause, I would have ensured this. But unfortunately, I was not on the Bench then. I did try to reopen the matter, but by the time it came up, I was retired.

'I am glad someone is looking into the matter now in whatever way. It needs a humane touch to it,' Justice Misra asserts.

Laws are laws, and there isn't much one can do if the victim is on the wrong side of the law, however unfair it is. But the thing that really upsets members of ACT and Pradeep in this particular case is the manner in which the Indian Embassy in the US dealt with this issue.

'They were in an extreme hurry to send her back to India. They did not study her case and it seems the Ambassador facilitated her travel documents so fast as if it was our duty to get her back. And this has been the weakest link in Jennifer's fight to return home,' says Pradeep.

And what could be the reason for this mad rush?

'No mind, much less its application by the Indian Embassy,' sums up Pradeep. 'In such matters the Ambassador should have taken legal advice rather than acting in utter haste.'

After running from pillar to post, Jennifer, on the advice of her lawyers, even appealed to President Obama to consider her case on humanitarian grounds.

38.

Seven months had passed since Jennifer was doing the graveyard shift at Leister.

One day, a new batch of trainees was being recruited at the centre. She and some of her colleagues looked down at the hall below at the new recruits just out of sheer curiosity. Amongst the trainees was a young boy in a blue and white checked shirt and jeans. Tall and lanky with a smooth, dark and shiny skin, he looked up and smiled at Jennifer when he caught her looking at him. She liked his smile and immediately smiled back. In fact, she liked smooth dark men. But this guy was not a man, more a young boy just out of his teens.

The next day, the young boy was assigned to sit next to Jennifer in her cubicle to 'barge her calls'. 'Barging in' takes place when a conversation with a client goes on for too long or a customer becomes too difficult to deal with, an operator or 'barger' comes in to divert/interrupt the call.

'Hi. I am Austin,' the lanky boy with a cute smile introduced himself.

'Hi Austin. I am Jennifer.'

'Oh.' Austin said as he sat next to her.

Work went on as usual and Jennifer started to explain a few things to Austin. After what seemed like a couple of hours' time, Jennifer wanted a smoke. She gestured to Austin that she was stepping out for a smoke. 'Can I join you Ma'am? I need a smoke too,' Austin replied.

'Yeah, sure. And the name's Jennifer. You can call me Jenny. No ma'aming me, understand?'

Austin's shiny face broke out into a wide smile. The two stepped out for a smoke.

'You smoke weed Jenny?' Austin, a quick learner asked curiously as he saw Jennifer rolling a joint.

'Yeah dude. Any problem with that?' Jennifer asked.

'Nope. I was just wondering if I could also have a couple of puffs. I need one badly.'

'Ah ha. I figured you were doing dope. Here, take a puff,' Jennifer extended her cigarette while Austin puffed at it like a veteran. Exhaling, he asked, 'Tell me Jenny, how long did it take you to get this American accent?'

'Whaddya mean? This ain't no accent man. This is how I speak. I am American.'

'Oh sure.' Austin smiled.

'You don't believe me, do you? I am an US citizen. From Chicago. Heard of Chicago?' Austin nodded.

'Then what are you doing here?' Austin asked.

'Got deported, man. Waiting to sort out my papers and go back soon. I should be home in another six months' time,' Jennifer lied, like she did to everyone in order to impress. 'Till then doing some time pass and earning some rupees instead of dollars,' she said.

'I see.' Austin seemed very impressed. And he believed her now.

And thus started their friendship, mainly bonding over weed.

One day, Austin offered to share his tiffin or dabba with Jennifer during the dinner break. He noticed Jennifer never got food from home and mainly snacked at the canteen. 'Hmm. This is yummy,' Jennifer said as she pigged into the simple fare of rice, dal and potato bhaji. 'Your mom made it?'

'Yes,' Austin replied. 'You live with your parents?'

'Yes. My mom, dad and my elder brother.'

'I see. And what does your family do?' Jennifer asked curious to learn more about Austin.

'My father is a driver with a company. My brother too is one. I have just finished my studies and this is my first job,' explained the twenty-two year old. 'My mother stays at home and looks after the house and cooks for us. She is a housewife.'

'And where do you live?'

'Thane. East. Near the railway station.'

❦

Over sharing meals and smoking up, Jennifer developed a liking for Austin though he was eight years younger than her. A young Chinese girl, who also worked in Leister, also took a liking to Austin and would tell everyone that she wanted him as her boyfriend. Jennifer was pissed with her though she was not vocal about it. She could not express her feelings for him because she felt people would find it weird as she was a lot older than Austin.

However, she knew Austin too had a liking for her when he asked her to be his date for his friend George's birthday party. Jennifer was very happy.

❦

'The party was at a hotel in Goregaon. There were more than twenty people. At first I felt a little odd amongst teenagers and twenty-year-olds. But then I had a good time and slowly got over my awkwardness.'

'But Austin was very good to me then. He was attracted to me. And guess what…I took his virginity at the party,' laughs Jennifer wickedly.

❦

39.

Austin Rozario belongs to a lower middle-class Maharashtrian family from Thane. 'We are pure Catholics,' Austin prides himself of his Roman Catholic background. Austin's father has been a 'company driver' for many years and his mother Julietta is a housewife. Austin has an older brother Sunny, who does odd jobs.

The first thing that attracted Austin to Jennifer was the fact she 'was a foreigner. I like foreigners and I like talking to them,' a trait which has seen Austin pushing drugs to such people in Goa. 'I liked Jenny's American accent and the fact that she lived in America for more than twenty years,' is how he sums up his first attraction for Jennifer. 'I was always interested in going to America and here was this American girl who was flirting with me...who knows she could take me to America with her and fulfil my dream. I don't want to stay in this country forever,' reminisces Austin. Little did he realize then that Jennifer Haynes could never ever be his ticket to the US.

'Initially, we were friends. Then one day she dressed up in a one-piece dress and had braided her hair and I knew she had done it for me,' laughs Austin. 'She started flirting and I flirted back...and...one thing led to another.'

The bond between Austin and Jennifer grew steadily. Apart from bonding over weed and dinner, Austin would also first drop Jennifer to Ghansoli and then detour back to Thane in the company car every morning after their shift was over. It set him back by an hour to reach home, but Austin did not mind.

Austin took the relation very seriously, 'more like a boyfriend–girlfriend business,' says Jennifer. Perhaps, this was because she was the first woman in his life. For her, he was more 'like a caring friend'.

Austin did not tell his mother about Jennifer initially. Instead, he would tell her that he was taking food for a friend and disappear from home for a couple of days to stay with Jennifer. Slowly, he confided to her that he was seeing a girl and much later introduced Jennifer to his mother. 'It is Indian society after all. We have to take one step at a time. Though my mother never objected to me having a girlfriend, she felt I was too young then and should concentrate on work more,' says Austin.

Meanwhile, Jennifer continued to share the digs with Rina and Sunny. Jennifer did not get along with them, and at the behest of Sunny, Rina extorted money from Jennifer. She was made to pay for food, which she never got, and excess electricity, which she did not use. 'Rina hardly gave me any food. By the time I reached home, Rina was away at work and by the time I left for work, Rina had not yet returned home. The only food that sustained me was Austin's dabbas.'

Many a time, Jennifer's money would be stolen at Rina's place, and she had to borrow money from the local grocer. And, when Austin started hanging around in the house, Rina objected. Austin however warned Jennifer that Sunny and Rina were taking her for a ride. Rina always spoke to the landlady and would not allow Jennifer to interact with her so Jennifer 'didn't exactly know what the rent was'. Later, Rina told her that the neighbours were objecting to Jennifer and Austin hanging around together since they were not married, and that she should vacate the place. Rina returned only five thousand rupees from her deposit, and Jennifer sold a few pieces of furniture given to her by Karen Sheikh, for three thousand rupees and shifted to a paying guest accommodation in Thane East, close to Austin's house.

After all these years and despite some bad blood with Rina, the two continue to share a close bond. She refutes Jennifer's charges of trying to cheat her or starve her. 'Jenny is hyper,' Rina concludes. 'The misunderstandings started with Austin. But whatever the reason, Jenny is a nice girl and continues to be my friend.'

On the other hand, for Austin, his relationship with Jennifer started 'more for fun' as he was really young at the time, but became serious when he learnt about the mess she was in. 'I felt bad for her and I wanted to help her out. And slowly I began to really like her…I started loving her. I felt I should help her out and I am grateful to God I was able to do that for her, even till today,' says Austin.

In Thane, Jennifer shared an apartment with four other girls. This was somewhere towards the end of 2012. She also worked in a call centre in Bhayander East for about six months. She would wait for Austin on her return from work, close to his house by a soda pop stall. When Austin underwent his circumcision, Jennifer stayed with him in the hospital. It was then that she met his family and came to know his mother, Julietta. The latter was not fond of Jennifer as she was possessive of her son like most Indian mothers. Also, she found Jennifer too old for her son.

Despite her initial reluctance about accepting Jennifer as her son's girlfriend, over time she began to tolerate her. In fact, both of them tolerated each other sharing a blow-hot-blow-cold relationship. Austin finds their relation very amusing. 'My mother and Jenny's relation is based on complete misunderstanding. Since my mother speaks only Marathi and Jenny only English, whenever my mother talks, Jenny feels she is abusing her. Whenever Jenny talks, my mother thinks she is making fun of her. I am the main go between them. And most of their misunderstanding starts whenever I am not around.'

※

When the other roomies were out at work during the day, Jennifer and Austin—both without jobs at the time—would use the premises to satiate their physical wants. Once, they had just had sex, when the agent came in and opened the door with her set of keys. On hearing the sound, Jennifer quickly sent Austin, who was stark naked, by the kitchen parapet and hid his clothes under the sofa. While the guests deliberated for twenty-five minutes, 'poor Austin was standing naked next to the hot pipes and getting fried!' Jennifer laughs recalling this.

Around this time, Jennifer got pregnant with Austin's child. But since neither of them was prepared to raise a child, Austin borrowed money from his mother and got Jennifer an abortion. Jennifer was not happy with this but she had no choice. 'If God gives you a life, we humans have no right to take it away. Bad luck followed me ever since,' says Jennifer.

After she left her job at the call centre, Jennifer was really hard of cash. She would steal clothes and toiletries from her roommates. Initially, she was warned but when she failed to listen, she was thrown out. She shifted out to a small room in Subhashnagar in Thane East, in an area called Khopri. Austin's mother, Julietta, paid the initial deposit of thirty thousand rupees and much to her annoyance, her son moved in with Jennifer.

Of course, the real reason behind Julietta paying the deposit and grudgingly accepting Jennifer as his son's girlfriend, was basically to keep a tab on her son. Austin was deep into peddling cocaine, weed, meth and MDA. He himself was doing meth and cocaine.

Austin also did not get along with his father in those days as he was always rebelling, as most youngsters do. He decided to move in with Jennifer. Jobless, he used to be away from home on days on end without any contact with his family. Julietta used to be worried stiff. She realized the only way to get to know about the whereabouts of her son was through Jennifer. So, she not only befriended her but also tolerated her tantrums. She decided to help Jennifer with her rent mainly to learn about Austin's whereabouts. Since he would stay with Jennifer, his mother could at least rest safe in that knowledge.

40.

Six months into the new place as a couple, both Austin and Jennifer were jobless. Jennifer got the boot from Epicenter for smoking weed while on the job. Austin's friends George and his girlfriend Leoda used to visit them most evenings. They all smoked a few joints together and sometimes had some rum and Coke or a cheap whiskey. Through the day the duo slept, woke up late and sometimes trooped into Austin's place for lunch or ate a sandwich. If Austin was in a good mood, he cooked for Jennifer. 'Austin's a good cook. Better than his mother who makes those lousy Maharashtrian dishes with curry leaves smothered in tomatoes. But I can't cook, leave alone make a cup of tea,' admits Jennifer.

Sometimes George brought along a guy called Salman, who sold drugs like weed and meth in a small way, locally. One day, Salman got his girlfriend Shruti, who hit it off with Jennifer. 'Shruti was a nice chick and we soon became friends. Unlike Leoda, who thought herself to be superior and moved around with hi-fi bitches who dressed stylishly,' says Jennifer sounding a little envious. 'But, George, of course, was a sweet guy and a good friend.'

'Shruti and I moved around a lot. She is well-educated and was studying hotel management. I think she must have completed her course now, though we are not in touch these days. She is actually from Goa. Of course, no one back home knew she was dating Salman as they would not approve of her seeing a Muslim boy. I remember one time when she was pregnant and we helped her deliver a baby boy in the backseat of a car. Later she gave the kid up for adoption. Looking at the skinny Shruti, you'd never think she could carry a baby.'

The six of them would hang around in Jennifer's pad smoking up every evening. They started out with weed and slowly with the entry of Salman, who was dealing in cheap meth, they started doing meth too.

Methamphetamine, or meth as it commonly known, is a strong central nervous system stimulant and is used as a recreational drug, mainly as an aphrodisiac and mood enhancer. Though in small doses it can elevate mood and alertness and also help in losing weight, in higher doses it can induce psychosis and cerebral haemorrhage.

Used for long periods it can affect the brain structure. It is illegally trafficked, mainly in the US, and is considered even deadlier than crack and heroin. It is costlier too.

The chemical structure of meth is $C_{10}H_{15}N$ and it is known by many names such as ice, chalk and crystal amongst other things. It is a white, odourless, bitter-tasting powder. The drug became popular amongst drug abusers when a popular American crime series, *Breaking Bad*, was aired on American television in 2008. It went into five seasons ending in 2013, having won a number of awards including the Emmy and Writers' Guild Award, besides becoming an all-time popular series on American television history, ranking thirteenth.

'Unlike in the US, where they use pure chemicals,' explains Jennifer, familiar with all kinds of substances, 'And it is very strong there. Here, it is much milder. But then they use shit here, literally dog shit, to make meth,' she laughs. 'It is bogus stuff. They use dog shit, metals from dead batteries and gasoline, which give the burning sensation, to make meth among other chemicals. As a result the side-effects are worse and it literally cuts through your nose-pipe and lungs. I would never suggest anyone to use meth. It is mighty dangerous.'

Initially, it was only Salman and George doing meth, while Salman also sold a little of it. Then they initiated Austin into using it and slowly he started getting hooked to it. Soon Austin became a meth addict. He started losing weight as his appetite shrunk, and Julietta blamed Jennifer for her son's failing health. Though in her heart she knew it was the drugs that were killing him. Just before he met Jennifer, Justin was peddling drugs in a small way. 'Mainly weed and grass locally. Later Salman, George and I became partners and we started selling weed and a bit of cocaine in Goa. It was more for fun then.'

According to Austin, though he started with weed and then graduated to cocaine and then meth and finally MDA, which according to him 'is even more potent than meth. With meth you only see stars, but with MDA you see the entire galaxy.'

It was after he started dating Jennifer that Austin started serious peddling. 'For a year in 2012–13, I was famous all over Thane, Ghansoli, Tubey and even as far as Kalyan and Ambernath for cocaine and weed. There were a number of cops from the crime branch who were aware of our activities but we were very discreet and also very smart. Three of us operated together. We normally supplied only to people we knew. In case a new customer called through our contacts, we were very cautious. We would call him at a public place, mostly train stations and we would check him out before meeting him. Sometimes, we would go to the station half an hour before and check his movements and if we had the slightest suspicion, we would leave.'

'We were especially wary of brown shoes and black shoes as they could be undercover cops,' laughs Austin. So while one of them did the trading, the other two looked out for danger. This was their modus operandi.

❦

One day Salman brought in his friend Sandeep who was the main supplier of meth. Sandeep was based in Byculla, from where he got his supply from a vendor who also made meth after adding his 'bogus' and cheap ingredients, which if used over a long period could even prove fatal. Sandeep would bring in a couple of friends and there would be nearly ten to a dozen people doing drugs in Jennifer's house every evening. 'My place became a rave joint. Every evening we would have rave parties. With psychedelic lights and all. Sandeep would supply Austin and me free drugs for using my place and others would bring in the booze and sometimes *chakna* (snacks). Sandeep would bring in his friends and buyers and obviously make money out of them,' recalls Jennifer. 'Sandeep was of course much older than us and doing well, selling meth. One day, I decided that instead of just them using my place as a rave joint and Austin just using meth, it was better we got some business out of it. He used to store boxes of the substance in my place.'

'Hey dude,' Jennifer asked Sandeep one day. 'What about giving me some of your stuff to sell?'

'Don't joke with me Jenny. You know it is dangerous. You are a woman and that too, a foreigner. You will not know what and how to sell. You will get everyone arrested,' Sandeep laughed.

'Listen carefully dude. I know what I'm saying. I have been peddling crack cocaine in Chicago, which is far more dangerous than your ch***a Mumbai. You understand. I know how to take care of myself. I know the business, man, trust me.'

Sandeep nodded hesitatingly. Jennifer continued, trying to impress upon him, 'Besides, man, you sell bogus stuff. Not even meth. At least with my American accent, people will think I am selling the real stuff. Imported stuff. Know what I mean? That way you will get more hi-fi clients. And good money. What say dude?'

'I can't take chance. Can't risk Jenny...' Sandeep started before she cut him short.

'Alright bh***i ki,' she said softly. 'No more entertaining clients in my place and no more coming here. No more keeping your bogus stuff here. You can clear right away you motherf***er or I call the police.'

Sandeep was shocked at the sudden turn of events. Salman and George tried to intervene, she pushed them away roughly. 'C'mon. Beat it guys. Fast.' When Austin tried to stop her, she told him off. 'These people take you for a ch***a. They make the money and use you and you make nothing but lie around like an addict. Can't you see their game plan? They are using us to get rich. It is time we made some money.' Turning to Sandeep and the rest she yelled, 'Out. Or I call police.'

'Okay. Okay. One minute Jenny. You win. You sell meth. Okay?'

'Okay.' Jennifer nodded. 'That's better dude.'

'But I give you only one chance. If you fuck up, then over. You understand? One chance.' Sandeep said.

'Yes man. I understand. And if I don't, then you take me in your gang. You understand?'

Austin was visibly impressed, his shiny countenance shinier. He had never seen Jennifer so bold before. He went and held her closer to him. Everyone clapped, sighing with relief. 'It's a deal then?' Jennifer extended her hand towards Sandeep.

'Deal,' Sandeep held her hand limply.

❦

Her first customer the following day was a guy called Rahul, one of Sandeep's contacts. She met him at Thane station and sold him two packets of meth for a thousand bucks each. They cost her that much for the entire amount. She made a cool fifty percent profit—one thousand rupees in just a few minutes. That was real easy money.

And, so started Jennifer's new career as a hustler in India. She was back to square one.

❦

She picked up most of her clients from the lot that came home. The rave parties continued daily, with psychedelic lights and loud music. On top of this there were loud noises made by the people, and at times couples like Salman and Shruti screaming at each other, drunk. This continued for a year till the neighbours started complaining. Meanwhile Jennifer had built up a steady clientele for meth and weed and did not need to depend on Sandeep for this.

Jennifer decided to vacate the place after her eleven-months lease was over. 'If I hadn't moved out, the police would have busted us. The neighbours were complaining and the police were getting suspicious and from experience I could sniff they were hot on our trail. So I moved out to another place, a little away and more interior from the station. Since it was not on the main road, the guys found it inconvenient and stopped coming. But I found my peace here,' smiles from her current abode.

41.

16 June 2014 was an important day for Jennifer. Not only was it Justin's birthday, it was also the day Kassana came to India to meet her mother. It was six years since Jennifer had last seen her daughter (aside of their Skype calls), and Kassana was five at the time of her deportation. She was now eleven.

The reason for Kassana's visit to India was because she was getting difficult, defiant and rebellious. Almost like Jennifer was at that age. She was having problems with her teachers in school as well as with her babysitters. She was abusive to them as well as Judy who really 'pissed her off'. Kassana felt neglected by Judy as she thought the latter always favoured her brother, who was much more manageable and controllable. So Judy and her teachers in school felt that if she visited her mother and spent some time with her, perhaps her defiance would lessen.

According to Jennifer, 'It was a big mistake.'

Jennifer and Austin took a non-AC train to Delhi and stayed at a small hotel. Once Kassana arrived, they stayed at the Holiday Inn and returned in an AC coach.

On first seeing the broad-boned girl who was a foot taller than her, Jennifer cried. She had left her as a small child back in Chicago. Now here was eleven-year-old young girl, who looked much older than her age! The petite Jennifer felt small next to her baby. When Kassana saw her mother, her first reaction was one of surprise. 'Mom, you are so small! So short! Mom, you are so little. I cannot believe you are my mom! And who is this kid with you?' she asked of Austin, who looked more her age than her mother's.

For Kassana, India was a culture shock. She would sulk. She hated the heat. And she would not let Austin touch her things. She ate all possible junk food and drank cans of sodas, that she vomited at first. 'I wanna go back to Meme,' she cried. Meme was Judy.

When she arrived in Mumbai, she hated Jennifer's 'digs'. She found it 'shabby' and 'dirty' and 'poor'. Initially, she hated George and the gang coming home and doing drugs. She was bored and complained to Judy a lot over Skype. But, slowly she got friendly with the gang. Since she hated Indian food of dal-rice-curry, Austin and George would feed her pizzas and burgers. She missed the beef burgers though.

Gradually, she opened up to Austin and got friendly with him. According to Jennifer, 'She even developed a little crush on him. Whenever Austin and I hugged, she would get jealous. She would resent it. I dunno whether it was her anger at Austin for touching her mom or at me for being close to him.'

'I also messed it up with us big time. Not being around with children and being on my own for such a long time, I had no idea what to do with Kassana. I could not give her quality time. She harboured a lot of anger for me because I didn't give her much love.'

'She made fun of my looks. She looked down upon my lifestyle, my dressing sense. The strange thing was I always wanted to go back home for my kids. But when my kid was here, I didn't know how to handle her,' admits a teary-eyed Jennifer.

Jennifer weighed the pros and cons and decided that 'Kassana would be better off there as I was leading a most uncertain life. So I deliberately did not smother her with love because I knew it would hurt when she left for the US. At one point Kassana wanted to stay on and study here, but I insisted she return. She realized that too. She was missing her friends. She left in October after spending four months with me. I couldn't say they were the best of times because we would fight a lot. There were ups and downs in our relation.'

When I first met Jennifer, Kassana was with her as she was visiting India at the time. The first impression I had of Kassana was she was ten going on twenty!

My teenage son seemed a lot younger than her.

Kassana was polite but not very forthcoming. She answered when asked, but did not volunteer much on her own. What struck me most was that she was quite confused about India and her mother. She seemed to be very confident when she was in her American space, be it television serials or junk food or gadgets. She was enjoying the fact that she was missing school but you could see she wanted to get back home. She was enjoying her time with her mother, but she was not sure whether to treat her mom like a sister or a mother or a friend. The confusion was apparent.

Kassana would go into mood swings but I knew she was trying her best to adjust to the circumstances. Both mother and daughter were making a sincere effort. But knowing Jennifer's mood swings and then Kassana's, I knew it was better for Kassana to live her own familiar life and I suggested this to Jennifer. What I figured was that Kassana was enjoying the attention she was getting here, away from her brother, but I knew this would not last forever.

Jennifer went into a mild depression after Kassana left. On 8 December, she bought a mixed breed pup from Crawford Market for three and a half thousand rupees. 'I was lonely and depressed. Spanie, my puppy baby, has been my steady companion ever since.'

42.

When Jennifer left her children, they were too young to realize the meaning of a 'mother'. Kassana was only three and Kadafi was four. For them it was their 'Meme' or grandmother, Judy Cobbs, who filled in for their mom. Their most important childhood milestones and memories were with Judy and not Jennifer. Besides, Justin having been away for most of the time, they did not have their father around too. So, it is but obvious they would look up to her as the most important person in their lives, and also the one who is mostly responsible for shaping their thoughts and values.

Although Judy did not herself come from happiest of families, she managed to build a life of respect and dignity for herself. Having educated herself and then building a career in a legal firm for years, it was obviously disappointing for her when her son got into hustling.

When Justin was courting Jennifer, Judy thought that Jennifer, 'a good girl who needed a family who could love her', would perhaps help her son change his ways. Then she hoped Justin would maybe later change his ways after having children. But sadly, that was not to be.

So, Judy was not just a grandmother to Kadafi and Kassana, she also ended up parenting them. And yet, all along she knew as well as the children that she was not their mother.

Initially, the children did miss their mother. They even drew pictures saying they were missing her and babbled about it over Skype. Soon, it became a matter of duty and routine as they gradually got involved in their own lives. Of course, somewhere they knew they had a mother and father who could not be with them like their friends' parents. And this upset them and affected their studies.

According to Judy, Kassana is social and outgoing while Kadafi is more reticent. 'Kassana has behavioural problems both at home and school and this is a real challenge, especially in school.' When it was beginning to affect her studies, Judy decided to send her to India. 'I thought being with her mom would help, instead it had the opposite effect.'

According to Judy, she was very unhappy in Mumbai, especially as she did not approve of her mother's life. But according to Jennifer, despite her initial uneasiness with creature comforts, Kassana loved all the attention Jennifer and Austin showered on her. 'She did not want to go back,' says Jennifer. Perhaps being difficult and being constantly compared with the gentle Kadafi, Kassana thought it would be better to stay on in India.

'Although Kassana is in therapy currently and we do what we can here at home for her, she continues to act out, especially in school,' says Judy. 'This has been posing problems for some time.'

As for Kadafi, she says, 'He doesn't have those problems but I'm always on him about his homework. For him at least right now, it's typical teen issues. He is liked in school and doesn't act out.'

Wouldn't Kadafi like to visit his mother in India?

'It would be nice for Kadafi to see his mom. But at the same time, I will not send him there. He didn't want to go when Kassana went. As you are aware Jennifer did not want to return Kassana. And I had to go through emotional hell to get her back,' explains Judy.

There was a huge fiasco regarding Kassana's return to the US. When I questioned Jennifer on this, she gives her version. 'Actually, though Kassana did not like it at first in India, she got used to it and then she began enjoying herself. Especially all the attention she got from Austin and me. For her it was like one long picnic. She did not want to go back. The first time she refused and cried. She missed the flight. The ticket was wasted and Judy was mad. It took her time to arrange the money for the next ticket. The next time Austin and I literally had to drag her out of the room and put her on the flight.'

'As for Kadafi, I am dying to hold him,' says Jennifer of her first-born. 'He does want to come to visit me during the holidays and spend a couple of months like Kassana did, but Judy says she has no money. Maybe she doesn't want to send him.'

※

Though Judy has stood by Jennifer through thick and thin, nevertheless she has changed her opinion of her. From the 'good girl who needed a family who could love her' Jennifer has gone on to become a 'liar and manipulative'.

'She doesn't tell the truth about herself or her current life and hides stuff from me. I am not close to her now and do not trust her at all, but I will continue to do things for her because I know she loved Justin and she is the mother of my grandchildren,' says Judy.

For someone who 'did not enjoy being a single parent' as she was forced to, Judy does not recommend it.

'I think a child needs both the father and mother. As far as a grandmother is concerned, I cannot really be that since I am raising the kids,' she smiles. 'It's not great either when you have a full-time job. I should be relaxing now,' says the senior citizen, who looks much younger than her years.

In order to de-stress from her 'intense full-time job' as well as managing two adolescent kids, she works out thrice a week at Orange Theory Fitness. 'It's a tough intense workout with those half my age. But I do quite well. When I first started out there was no one my age but that was quite okay coz I was doing it along with my routine life. Then people my age started working out. We are all in it to win. It is a way to get way and reduce stress,' explains Judy on her way of nurturing herself to good health.

'Despite all her actions, I know all that Jenny has been through enough. I can only empathize. She is the one who went through all the shit. The only solution I see to Kadafi and Kassana's problems is if their mother being back here with them. These are times when they need her most even if adjusting with them will take a while. But then only a miracle can make that happen,' rues Judy.

When I ask Judy to speak to Kadafi and Kassana about their mother and their feelings for her now, Judy tells me, 'With regard to the children, I wish to protect their privacy of thoughts as it relates to their mother. I will pose your questions to them though.'

Kassana refused to say anything about her mother as she and Jennifer are not on the best of terms currently.

As for Kadafi, he agreed to answer the questions.

How do you feel about your mom?
I feel my mother is a great person and I still love her even though she went away.

Do you want to see your mom?
Yes.

Do you like talking to your mom on the phone?
Yes.

If you could say anything to your mom right this minute, what would you say?
I love you.

Do you remember your mom in Michigan?
Yes, well actually I don't remember a lot, but I remember she was there.

Is there something else you would like to say?
No. Oh, I like how she tells me stories.

What do you mean stories?
She tells me stories about when I was little.

Is there anything else you want to say?
No.

43.

Year 2018. It has been nearly a decade since Jennifer has been living in India—the country of her birth, but one that was completely alien to her. She has been nurturing hopes from day one that she is here only temporarily, and that she would leave as soon as her papers were sorted. However, after all these years that was not to be. Even then, her hopes of returning, have not died down yet. She continues to live in a limbo. But, life goes on.

A typical day in Jennifer's life in her one-room tenement in Thane starts as early as 5 a.m. nowadays. The reason being, Austin has to report to work at 7 a.m. He has been working in small hotel called Ferns in Chembur as a front desk executive. According to Jennifer, she has managed to get him 'clean from meth', and it has been more than a year since he has stopped doing meth and held on to his job. Had it not been for Austin's morning shifts, Jennifer's day would only begin around noon.

After seeing Austin off to work at 6 a.m., Jennifer rolls back into bed with Spanie and does not wake up before 11–11.30 a.m. Jennifer is not a breakfast person and at most, she has a canned juice and two cigarettes for breakfast. Though she loves tea, she does not know how to make masala chai. 'When Austin is home he makes masala chai for me,' she says. If she feels very hungry, then she goes across to Julietta's for a lunch of dal and rice, but she does not savour the typical Maharashtrian food. 'I find it too spicy and boring,' she says. Else she sits and watches television.

Since there is water rationing, she waits for water to come around 5 p.m., when she does her washing and cleaning and saves some potable water for the day. Around 5.30 p.m., she goes to her neighbour's for a coffee with ginger. 'Eeeks!', she laughs at my reaction. 'I know it is a weird combination, but that's the way she has it and I have kinda got used to it. Besides, it's food for the throat,' she adds by way of a limp explanation.

After catching up on neighbourhood gossip, she takes Spanie for a stroll and has a cigarette. Once home around 8 p.m., she goes back to the television, which she considers her lifesaver. Austin returns from work around that time but he spends a couple of hours with his folks and comes home with a dabba at around 9.30–10 p.m. The dabba is their dinner.

Normally, they smoke a joint together before dinner. By 11 p.m. the couple retires. 'Before going to bed, I read a little from the Bible to him,' says Jennifer, a Catholic by birth. And that is how she likes to end the day. With a little introspection. And a thank you note to the Lord Almighty.

※

She has adapted to India and its local customs and culture. Jennifer manages to travel on her own from one end of the city to the other and even beyond. She has even travelled to Goa for a bit of hustling. Though she is not conversant in Hindi, the main language of communication here, she manages to find her way around and mostly understand the spoken word. But what she has mastered most is her use of cuss words. 'Having to deal with the illiterate and lower strata of society and the druggies and dealers, this is the lingo they are familiar with and understand. Or else it becomes difficult to get work out of them,' she explains.

It is amazing the way she uses Indian cuss words with an American accent while integrating it with English without batting an eyelid. One would think it was a part of the English language. If Jennifer had her way, these words would soon be part of the Oxford English Dictionary!

The first time I visited her abode in Thane and was looking for a place to park my car at the station, she called out to the parking attendant, 'Hey m*d*r***d [motherf***er], get us a parking na.' The attendant immediately obliged. But my 'boyfriend', who accompanied me, looked shocked. Another time when we visited the Fatima Church at Ambernath, she yelled at an auto rickshaw driver who was blocking our path, 'Hey bh**ri (c*nt), move it you ch*t*a (f**k*r).' The guy immediately obliged, before what she said sank in. This time my 'boyfriend' blushed with embarrassment.

Sometimes it's the other way round. She speaks with American words thrown in, and even they are not cuss words, they are however alien to the Indian milieu. People look rather shocked. The other day while buying a pair of shoes, she realized she needed a size larger. She asked the salesman, 'Dude, give me a size bigger na.' The salesman blushed at being called a 'dude' and obliged with a smile.

Though her relationship with Austin is mostly blow-hot-blow-cold and not exactly like a romantic couple but more like 'buddies'. Jennifer is very fond of him. She may call him a 'motherf***er' or 'chu**a' from time to time, but she says, 'I would do anything for him. He brought me food when I most needed it. He was there for me in a strange land when I had nobody. He is the only true friend I have despite our quarrels.'

'I know I am married and cannot marry him. We have been in a relationship for three years now but I still find him a kid. I want him to marry a nice Indian girl someday. And someday, I hope to return to Justin. Despite his live-in girlfriends, I still love Justin, as he is the father of my children. And if and when I return to the US, if I can take Austin with me to get him a better future there, I would love to do it.'

Perhaps one of the reasons for her not wanting to settle down with Austin is because of his childish nature. She recalls the time two years ago on Friendship Day the gang of friends went to Jughead's at Thane. At the diner, Austin, high on meth, spoke about Jennifer in a derogatory manner in front of his friends. 'I didn't like that.' Not one to give in easily, she took a stick and 'beat the shit out of him. He kept his trap under control since then.'

More than Austin, she also has a troubled relation with his mother. 'Mentally Julietta is all messed up. She is too controlling of her son,' says Jennifer. 'Initially, she resented me outright and told me to stay away from her son. I told her to keep her son off my ass,' she says. 'Once I told Austin about her rudeness, he told her off. Ever since, she keeps a distance from me. Sometimes she pretends to love me, but I know it is only a charade. She does it to keep a tab on her son and the only way she can do this is to get information from me. But one day I told her point blank that I did not want to marry her son. Her husband barely talks and Austin's older brother is also on his own trip. Julietta wears the pants in the house.'

However, when she is in an expansive mood, she says Julietta has been very kind to her and a lot of their misunderstandings stem from their language barrier.

✼

Of late, Jennifer has been desperately looking for a job. It has been nearly a year now that she gave up hustling. Sometimes twice, sometimes thrice, Jennifer comes all the way from Thane, changing trains twice to sit with me over her story for the book. 'You know dude,' she tells me. 'Since the Supreme Court has rejected my plea, I am depending on you and this book to get me back home on humanitarian grounds,' she says with implicit faith. 'And I decided to come clean. Hustling is easy money. I have my fixed clients. Plus some others. Some months I make twenty grands and at other months it goes up to fifty. But if I get caught, then I get jailed. And then the purpose of this book will fail. There will be no fucking sympathy for me. And besides, I don't wanna land up in an Indian jail, man! Holy sh*t!'

While she has seen to it that Austin sticks to his job by getting up at 5 a.m. to 'shove his ass out of the house,' she also is proud that she has managed to 'make him come clean of meth'. 'He only does weed now, and that too in mild doses,' she says. 'And he has managed to stick around in Ferns for nearly a year now.'

'I have also given up hustling since the past year.'

However, life has not been easy for Jennifer ever since.

There is no money. There is no job. She has been going for job interviews. She is not picky anymore. From call centres to receptionists at a factory in Thane to a doctor's chamber in Andheri to a mall in Mulund as a salesgirl, she has tried it all. But no one seems to want her. Either her 'accent is too American', or she 'doesn't speak any local language', or 'she is shabbily dressed'—there is no dearth of excuses.

Sangeeta Punekar's words come to mind: 'Jennifer does not belong here. Since she was sent out as a child for adoption to the US, it is the responsibility of the US government to organize her papers. And when they deported her, the Indian government should have sent her back. That way, by now she would have got her US citizenship, served her term and been with her children, leading an honest life.'

I will go a step further and add that now that we have taken her in, an American and therefore a guest, it is the duty of the Indian government to treat her like one. And, yet, we treat Jennifer like a piece of sh*t.

The least the Indian government can do is give her a small, decent place to stay and a minimum monthly allowance so that she can sustain herself by way of food, clothes and medicines, even if she is not working. Given her mental and emotional condition, Jennifer is not able to sustain jobs for long. It is the Indian government's duty and responsibility to take care of her basic needs.

Currently, she is surviving on the goodness of friends and well-wishers. Austin contributes a part of his meagre salary of eight thousand rupees towards the rent. Some friends pitch in with some money for her daily needs. Julietta, despite her animosity towards Jennifer, provides her with food and sometimes helps her out with money to buy essentials. Jennifer just about manages to survive.

'I am not living. I am surviving,' she says.

44.

'Hey Jenny, I am happy Austin is working. Good job. You wake up early and take trouble to send him to work. You wake very early. So much trouble for you. I want to thank you for helping my Austin keep his job,' Julietta told Jennifer one day as she handed her a fifty rupee note. Every month, Julietta gives Jennifer fifty rupees without fail. This is for her sanitary napkins.

'You're welcome. Thank you also for helping me. You feed me, sometimes you help with my rent and all these little things you do for me,' Jennifer said holding up the fifty bucks.

A couple of months later as Jennifer was lazing and watching TV at Austin's house with Julietta one afternoon, after they lunched on dal-rice and fried *bhangra* fish, Julietta suddenly said, 'Jenny, all okay na?'

'Meaning?'

'All okay with you?' Julietta persisted.

'Why shouldn't it be?' Jennifer asked surprised.

'I mean you and Austin...' she indicated by crossing her two forefingers.

'Me and Austin what?'

'You and Austin, having relations na...?'

'Ask your son. Don't ask me,' Jennifer sounded curt.

Jennifer

'No. I don't mean that. I mean all okay with you na...?' Julietta hesitated.

'Why shouldn't it be?' Jennifer retaliated.

'Because last two months you didn't ask for pad money.' She meant sanitary napkins.

'Oh that,' Jennifer suddenly realized that she had not got her periods for two months. She was a little worried but did not want to let Julietta know about it. 'Arrey, I had some money with me. George had given. So it's okay. Don't worry. Chill.'

The next day she had come to Versova, a swanky suburb of Mumbai and a good 70-odd kilometres from Thane for some work. She went to a chemist's and picked up a pregnancy kit, satisfied that no one would know her in this area. On returning to her pad, she bolted herself in and did the pregnancy test. The results were positive. Jennifer was stunned.

While Justin was in prison, Jennifer had had a one-night stand with an African American guy and got pregnant. Being a Catholic, it was against her religion to abort. Despite Judy offering to adopt the baby, Jennifer realized it would not be feasible with two small children. Besides, Justin was upset. So, she aborted the baby.

The second time around when she got pregnant by Austin while living as a paying guest in 2012, neither of them were prepared to raise a child, so she had the baby aborted again. And now she was in a quandary. 'The last time I dropped the baby, bad luck followed Austin and me for two years. It continues to follow. I didn't know what to do. I just kept the news to myself,' says Jennifer.

A few days later, Jennifer went to Julietta and asked her for fifty rupees. 'You got your periods na?' Julietta asked smiling, albeit a little suspiciously.

'No. Austin's got periods,' Jennifer replied cheekily.

'No, no. I meant, so suddenly now?'

'Actually my periods gave me a warning a month ago that "I am coming dear."'

Julietta handed her a fifty rupee note, muttering, 'Why you are rude to me? I didn't mean that...' Jennifer had already left. She headed straight to the store and bought herself a canned juice and two cigarettes, her daily fix.

※

Next day it was Austin's off day. He and Jennifer decided to have lunch at his parents'. Julietta made her son's favourite meal—dal-rice and fried *bhangra* fish. Jennifer also liked the combination. A little after lunch, Jennifer went to the little bathroom and puked. All along Julietta eyed her suspiciously.

The next afternoon while Austin was away at work, Julietta called Jennifer and asked her over for lunch. 'I am making chicken biryani. I know you like it Jenny. Come for lunch.'

'I'll have it for dinner with Austin. Now I am feeling tired. I want to sleep.'

'Are you alright Jenny?'

'Yes. Just tired.' She hung up.

※

Twenty minutes later there was a knock on her door. Jennifer opened to find Julietta standing there with a small steel box. 'I was worried. You did not sound well. You must eat or you will feel weak. That's why I got you biryani,' she said, handing her the meal box.

'I told you I am tired. I want to sleep,' Jennifer was irritable.

'It is okay. You eat first. Then sleep. Or you will feel weak,' Julietta sounded unduly concerned as she patted Jennifer on her butt. 'You said you got periods. Then why aren't you wearing a pad?' asked the clever lady.

'Arrey, my period is over,' Jennifer replied, taken in by complete surprise. She knew Julietta had her suspicions and was checking her out.

'How come? You took money three days ago?'

'Yeah. Nowadays I bleed for only a day. Getting old,' Jennifer explained. Julietta did not seem very convinced though she nodded her head half-heartedly as she left.

※

The next day Jennifer had made up her mind to keep the baby come what may. She broke the news to Austin. Austin shrugged and said, 'We'll have to drop the baby.' For the first time Jennifer put her foot down strongly, 'Who are you to decide you motherf**er? It is my baby and I will decide.'

'But how will we raise the baby? I don't have a permanent job. You don't have any work. We are not married. How can we marry and have a child if there is no money? I am not prepared...'

'Remember the last time I dropped our baby?' Jennifer cut Austin off. Austin nodded. 'It was panauti [ill-luck]. Misfortune followed. I will not drop the baby this time.'

'I do not want your support. I am not asking you to take any responsibility. You continue with your life, I will with mine. I will raise this baby on my own. If I cannot manage financially, I will give it up for adoption. If God has given a life, we humans have no right to take it away,' Jennifer said, 'You f**k off before I beat the sh*t out of you.'

Austin fled.

※

Next day Julietta came and told Jennifer to get an abortion. 'I will pay for it,' Julietta said, adding, 'I had my suspicion and that is why I asked you. You lied.'

'I am not getting an abortion,' Jennifer was firm.

'Then what will people say? The neighbours? The relatives?'

'F**k them,' Jennifer said.

'I have to live with them. If you are not getting an abortion then better you and Austin marry. Though I don't like you as a daughter-in-law, I want you to marry Austin for the baby's sake,' Julietta said.

'And what makes you think I want to marry your son?' Jennifer said. 'I don't want any marriage,' unable to disclose to Julietta that she was already married in the US to Justin. The Rozarios are under the impression that Jennifer is a divorcee.

'In that case,' Julietta said, 'you cannot stay in the neighborhood. People will talk. You go to another area and raise the child on your own. We have nothing to do with it.'

Saying this, Julietta stormed out. Neither mother nor son was supportive of Jennifer's decision.

It broke her heart. Jennifer had at least hoped that Austin would, if not physically, emotionally and morally support her. She decided to move out of Thane. She gave away her pet rabbits to a friend. She packed her stuff and took Spanie with her and moved to Rina's at Ghansoli. Since she never got along with Rina's husband, she asked Jennifer to stay in the salon instead. She and Spanie moved in to Rina's parlour this time.

A few days later Austin arrived at Rina's. 'He wanted Spanie and me home. He said Julietta was missing Spanie. They love Spanie a lot. Besides, it was no fun staying at Rina's as she was getting hassled and irritable. I decided to return to Thane.'

'I know Austin called me back because of Spanie. They don't give a rat's ass about me.'

'I don't know what's gonna happen in the future. What will I do with the baby? Will I be able to raise it? If I go back to the US,

I will definitely take it along with me. I will have enough support there with Judy.'

'And if I don't go back and cannot manage the baby here, I will give it up for adoption. But come what may, I will not drop the baby this time.'

Maybe it is Jennifer's way of catching up on her lost years of motherhood.

Whatever the cost Jennifer had decided to keep the baby. Despite friends persuading her otherwise, taking into account her poverty and hand-to-mouth existence, she still wanted to go ahead with the pregnancy. 'Who knows, the baby might bring me good luck! Since I don't see any hope for the future of returning to the US or to my children, at least I have someone to belong to. I see this baby as a hope for my future, a reason for living.'

45.

'Hello,' a voice said as I picked up my phone. It was Julietta. 'I want to talk about Jenny.'

'Yes,' I said apprehensively. 'Tell me.'

'You know na...about her condition?' Julietta said, obviously referring to her pregnancy.

'Yes.' I said curtly.

'I know she is very upset. And rightly so. What can I do?'

'What do you mean?' I said. 'Julietta please explain. I cannot follow you.'

'I have been trying to convince Austin that he should marry Jenny since he is responsible. Our religion does not permit abortion. And the neighbours are always gossiping. Therefore I told Jenny to shift out to another neighbourhood. But I feel bad about her. She is all alone. And now with the baby coming...' she broke off.

'Austin doesn't listen to me. He says he is too young to be burdened with responsibility. He has ambitions. He wants to go places. Maybe you could convince him to marry Jenny.'

I was stunned into silence. 'But I thought you did not like Jenny,' I barely whispered it out.

'Oh no, no, no. I know Jenny must have told you. Stupid girl. She is very hyper always. Always losing her temper and not understanding me. I don't know English and she does not know Marathi and she thinks I am always abusing her.'

'Never mind what she says about me, I am very fond of her. When I had my surgery, she stayed with me in the hospital and looked after me more than a daughter would. I know she does not show it but she loves me a lot. That is why I pamper her with her favourite fish curry often.'

'Besides, she is responsible for bringing my son back on track. I had lost him to drugs for some years. His health had also deteriorated with drugs. I always feared that if the police did not catch him some day, he would be dead from the drugs. Jenny has got him out of drugs and made him stick to his job. She is responsible for giving a new life to Austin.'

I was almost in tears. Julietta, a simple, illiterate woman, knew the value of a good human being. And what amazed me was that someone like Jennifer, who has been given such a raw deal by life and fate, has, despite her woes, managed to help someone out of his mess. It is because of the Jennifers and Juliettas of the world that I still have faith in mankind.

And most surprising of all is that a hustler of cocaine has actually got an addict to kick the habit. That is saying a lot.

I promised Julietta I would do my best.

When I spoke to Austin, he seemed a little wary of marriage. Not because he did not love Jennifer. 'I love her very much,' he emphasizes. 'It is just that I want to do something with my life. Maybe go to America,' he smiles.

When I ran this conversation with Jennifer and told her about Julietta's wish, she was very touched. 'But tell me in all honesty Jennifer, do you love Austin?'

'Yes I do. Very much.'

'And would you like to get married to him?'

Breaking into a smile she nodded, 'I do.'

※

I put Jennifer in touch with my gynaecologist Dr Veena Shinde, who not only ran the tests to see if the baby was doing fine, but also gave her a part-time job as a receptionist in her clinic between 6 p.m. and 10 p.m. on weekdays. The job included a dinner and the timings suited Jennifer just fine.

After settling down in her new job, she sent me a text one day:

Hi. How r u? I just got off work, I was thinking about u today. I really miss u man…miss my friend.

※

On 1 February 2018, Jennifer sent me a text at 2 a.m.:

Hi Nandita. I wanted to inform u that the baby died. The water had got busted and inside was dried up.

I saw it at 6 a.m. It was quickly followed by another message:

Ok, the baby came out 2 hours ago. Dead. I'm ok. Just a little sad.

Well, maybe it was nature's way of helping her out of her current situation without making her feel guilty.

When I reached the hospital, Austin had just left for home to shower. If Jennifer was sad, she did not show it. Seeing me she smiled and after a while asked, 'When are these b*h*nch**s gonna release me. I wanna go home, man.'

I laughed. This was the Jennifer I know. And this is the Jennifer, who, despite all the adversities in her life, is still swimming against all tides and bobbing her head up with a smile on her face.

I knew Jennifer would be fine again and ready to face the world soon.

Though she was back on her feet in a few days' time, she did not go back to work at Dr Shinde's. She sent me a text with an explanation:

> Nandita, I'm not ready to see pregnant women. It's starting to affect me now.

❧

A few days later Jennifer was back in my pad. She did not ask for alcohol or go out for a smoke. Her few months of coming clean during her pregnancy continued.

'Hey I got a job, man. At a call centre, 15 minutes from where I live. Isn't that cool? It's for a food chain express. It's really big in the US. And they're paying me fifteen grands…no joke. I join from day after,' Jennifer was all excited.

A few days later when I messaged her how she was enjoying her new job, she messaged back:

> Hi. I don't have a job now…the company verified me on Google and my story appeared there…they took me in without a school certificate but I didn't tell them my story…I want that story removed from Google, man, coz it's really messing my life.

So there it is. Jennifer—back where she started. Back to square one. The 'same old shit'.

❧

46.

There is a saying, 'If life throws lemons at you, make lemonade out of them'. This is something we all have been doing. Unfortunately, in Jennifer's case, life has thrown a whole lot of rotten lemons at her, not worth making lemonade with. Then what does one do?

And the worst was yet to come.

The miscarriage had dealt her a severe psychological blow. Not only did she feel 'that God had been very kind and it was a miracle I could have two beautiful babies. But going back to weed and misusing his kindness, God decided to take away this gift from me. Maybe I would never have a child again,' rues Jennifer.

Despite her unstable financial condition, she used to be excited during her early days of pregnancy. Though Judy and Justin did not approve of it, Judy nevertheless gave her moral support all the way from Chicago. 'Go ahead Jenny. I am with you,' she assured her. Though Justin was disapproving at first, soon after her miscarriage he called her at regular intervals, telling her to be careful in future like a concerned friend.

Jennifer's few calls to Judy went unanswered for a while despite her leaving messages on her voicemail. 'Hey Kadafi,' said Jennifer as Kadafi answered the call at Judy's Chicago home. 'Where's Judy? Been trying to reach her. She's not answering. Tell her I called her and to call me back,' Jenny told her son. 'And so how's my baby…' and thus continued the rest of the conversation.

A few days later when she didn't hear from Judy, she called up her home again. It was Kadafi again on the phone. 'Hey honey. Where's Grannie? I wanna talk to her.'

'Oh, she's gone out,' Kadafi said.

'Out? It's 7.30 a.m. for God's sake! Where would she go out so early? Besides, she has to get you guys ready for school,' Jennifer asked.

'Yeah. I know. We are getting ready to go to school. Grannie's been going out real early frequently. She says she's going to the doctor,' Kadafi explained.

'Doctor? What for? What's with her?'

'I dunno. She doesn't tell though we keep asking her. I guess she must be ill and it must be some serious illness. That's why she is not telling us,' Kadafi was almost crying on the other end.

'Relax, baby,' Jennifer tried to calm him. She was worried.

When Jennifer did manage to speak to Judy a few days later, the latter informed her that it was nothing much except for some routine tests. 'All okay, Mom?' Jennifer asked.

'Yes. All okay.' Judy was tight-lipped.

After subsequent calls when Jennifer found out that Judy was still away in the mornings, Jennifer could hold the suspense no longer and confronted Judy on the phone one day. 'You will have to tell me what the matter is. I ain't taking no for an answer.'

It was then Judy broke down and admitted she was undergoing treatment for a fatal illness. 'Oh my God!' was all Jennifer could say as her whole world came crashing down.

It was not only the question of who would take care of her children should anything happen to Judy, it was also the close bond that she built with Judy over the years, despite their disagreements. The news shook her.

Judy was the strongest support she had. The mother she never had. The mother-in-law who always supported her, even going against her own son at times. The friend who gave her sane counsel and helped her out of many a tight spots. And most important of all, the grandmother to her children who is a single parent to both.

'Should anything happen to Judy, I can see the world coming to an end for Kadafi and Kassana. They will be put in state foster care because Judy's husband, Jesse, is no way gonna look after them. They are not even his biological grandkids. Justin's away for another twenty odd years.'

'I dread to think what will happen if Kadafi and Kassana go to foster care. The same shit that happened to me. Coz foster care is one big bullshit there...I pray that even my enemies don't go there. Jail's a whole lot better, man.'

※

'Look dude,' Jennifer asked Aktoober Singh, the travel agent, running a small agency from Versova, called Super Deluxe Travel & Trade, 'You get me to the US.'

'Sure Ma'am,' the young Sardar smiled, 'Just tell me when and I will book your tickets. You need to get me your passport. I hope you have a visa Ma'am or else I will have to get one for you...'

Before Aktoober could complete his sentence, Jennifer cut him short. 'Look man, I can't get a US visa even though I have my passport.'

'Why?'

'Because I have been deported. I cannot fly back to the US, you understand?'

'Then?' Aktoober nodded without understanding.

'I'll have to go by boat,' Jennifer said matter-of-factly. Aktoober's jaw dropped.

'By boat! I don't understand. How can you go to the USA by boat?' he exclaimed.

'Look here,' Jennifer said as she pulled out a newspaper cutting and showed him. 'Look how all these men from Punjab are going to the US via South America. See here,' she explained to Aktoober 'The boats leave from Delhi and go to Brazil, then Equador, Colombia, Panama, Costa Rica, Honduras, Guatemala and then Mexico. And from Mexico I will enter the US without visa. It will be illegal, but that's okay. When the law doesn't help you, you gotta help yourself, man,' Jennifer concluded.

'Ma'am, it's not...'

'Don't worry, dude. I know it's a tough journey. Its gonna take a few months to reach Mexico by boat from India...but what the hell is another few months compared to eight years that I have waited to get back?' Jennifer cut him in.

'Ma'am, you are not understanding. It is not a question of a few months. The boats don't take women as it is a difficult and dangerous journey. It is only for men, no women allowed. The rough and tough Jat farmers from the *pinds* of Punjab. The villagers. They are used to hardships. Only they can bear it. Even then, many die. Like I know an aunt's sister-in-law's son, Charanjit. He drowned when the boat capsized near Panama.'

'And besides, Ma'am, I don't deal with such arrangements. I have a friend, Daljit. He deals with these arrangements, but then it will cost 2 or 3 lakh rupees. Also, he will not deal with women,' Aktoober informed.

It was not only the horrors of the journey that deterred her, but also arranging the huge sum of money, that put to rest Jennifer's plans of entering the US illegally.

※

Desperate to reach home at any cost, she even contemplated crossing over to the US through the Canadian border and at one time even via the Niagara Falls in a raft. All these were really far-fetched and risky, but when you are desperate, nothing matters.

When she shared these thoughts with Judy one day, the latter reprimanded her. 'I will be fine, Jenny. The medicines are working and I should recover soon. Just pray.'

And pray Jennifer does, despite having enough excuses to lose faith in life and prayers. 'Prayers and hope is all I have left now,' she says.

※

One day, Judy called Jennifer. 'You know Jenny, I have been thinking.

At some point, the children will need their mother. I am not keeping too well and I could do with some support and help. Besides, there is no hope for Justin's release in the immediate future. I was thinking of liquidating my savings and moving to Canada. The children can go to school there and will not feel too displaced from the US. Then you can join us there. We will have to start life afresh there.'

Jennifer was both surprised and touched. 'But what about Jesse?' Jennifer asked. 'Will he agree?'

'I don't know,' Judy said. 'It is all up to him.'

Jennifer could see Judy distressed at the thought of leaving her family, her relations, her husband and her life and starting afresh in the august years of her life, all so that Jennifer could be happy. 'I didn't want to displace her at this time of her life,' is all Jennifer says.

'But maybe in the future, I am not ruling out the possibility. But as of today, it is status quo.'

47.

I had retired for the day and almost dozed off when my cell phone pinged. I looked at my phone and saw a long message from Jennifer on WhatsApp. Thinking it could be one of her mood swings or perhaps a hate message targeted at me, I decided to handle the matter the next day instead of losing precious sleep over it. By now I had figured out Jenny's nuances.

Over my morning cuppa, I looked at Jenny's message. She wrote:

> Nandita this is what Judy sent me about Kassana. I don't know what to do. You are the only friend who came to mind. Nandita I am so sad inside to hear about my daughter.

I read Judy's message. It said:

> Kassana was singing an obscene rap in class with another girl repeating after her. They both were removed from class today.

The next one read:

> Kassana is who she is and I can't handle her. I am too old for her. Kassana is welcome to stay here but she has to be [sensible] about it...and she is not. She needs more than I can give her... she is your daughter not mine...I only got the kids by default. If she behaved in school, I could have handled...but she has got into wrong company and [is] leader of a girls gang, singing obscene rap songs in school. The teachers are mighty upset. I am too old now and if Kassana would behave it was okay...but I don't want to create a burden on you...but she is your child and she would be better off with you. I can only help a little and trust me that ain't much. Homeschool her or whatever. Do your best. She is coming. You won't be lonely.

And the last one read:

> I am a mother figure to Kassana and she doesn't appreciate it. Shows no respect. She is just like Justin and you. You must figure it out. It's your job now. I am not going to tell her now but I will bring her this summer and you take over her life.

To be honest, I didn't know how to react. Jennifer had wanted her children, even one of them to be with her. But she and I both knew that she wouldn't be able to handle them, especially Kassana, who was a rebel in every way. Also seeing Jennifer's financial state, I was wondering, how she would manage. I called her and we decided to meet.

Over a kebab biryani at the local diner, I asked Jenny what her reaction was to Judy's plans. 'I understand Judy's problem. But look at the state I am in. Besides, Kassana is not easy to handle, she's going to give me grief, man,' Jenny explained while nibbling on the long grains of rice.

'It's time you got some grief. Some responsibility. You have always wanted to go back to your children, at least one of them is coming to live with you...'

'You're right dude,' Jenny cut me off. 'I have been thinking about that too. Kassana will give me a reason to be anchored. I will have a routine life. I will have responsibilities. Instead of just faffing around all day and getting stressed. And somebody to live for, somebody to call my own.'

'Exactly,' I said.

'Except, I worry I will not be able to give her the life she's been used to.'

'Oh, all that will fall into place. She will get her mother...and despite all the misgivings, she will be near you.'

'Yes, I guess you are right.' Jenny's dark face crinkled into a smile.

'But I hope she stays on.'

'I hope she does,' I said.

'And who knows, Kadafi will also come and spend his holidays with us and maybe the children will love India. After all they are part Indian too, like their mother,' Jennifer admitted at last to her Indian roots.

'Know what dude, I'll slog my ass off for them. They'll be better off here with their mother, however poor, than in the American foster care homes.'

'Precisely,' I smiled seeing Jenny happy. At last, perhaps things were moving in the right direction.

I guess, even rotten lemons can be used to make lemonade provided you know how to separate the good from the bad part.

48.

Despite Pradeep Havnur and ACT along with Arun Dohle and Anjali Pawar, having tried their best to send Jennifer back to the US to be with her family—and Jennifer's longing to return home—little has been achieved till date. With the rejection from the Bombay High Court and then the Supreme Court, all hopes have dimmed for Jennifer. However, Pradeep has not given up hope. He insists that he will go for a repeal in the Supreme Court. Arun is also looking at other ways to get Jennifer to return to the US. Perhaps, on humanitarian grounds. Perhaps by finding loopholes in US immigration laws.

Jennifer's case is bizarre. Here are some expert opinions on the case from people associated with this matter, directly or indirectly.

Pradeep Havnur
Senior Lawyer
Once an inter-country adoption is approved and the child is sent out to another country by a High Court order, the child is no longer an Indian citizen. What I fail to understand is why the Indian Embassy in the US gave the travel documents to Jennifer to travel to India. Once a person has left after being adopted, and even if the adopting country does not give her citizenship, she loses the right to citizenship of the country from where she came from. In Jennifer's case, it was the callousness of the officials from the Indian Embassy who represented by the then Ambassador Meera Shankar, who, due to the non-application of her mind, blundered on this matter. It was much worse than death penalty for Jennifer.

Subsequently, the Supreme Court has passed an order whereby CARA has to ensure from the adoption agency of the country where the child is to be and accord the citizenship of that country before he/she steps out of India.

Monisha Cohelo
Human Rights Lawyer

If you are not a US citizen by birth, but a naturalized one, like in the case of this girl Jennifer Haynes, then you can be deported for certain serious crimes like tax evasion and certain crimes of moral turpitude. Only if you are a US citizen by birth, are you exempted from this.

Arun Dohle
Human Rights Worker
Founder Member, ACT

Her deportation is totally unjustified. The chances of her return are slim. It would require serious litigation in the US and huge funds. She has aggravated felony charge against her above the non-citizenship status, so it is quite complicated.

Currently, we are part of the Adoptee Rights Campaign (ARC) initiated by Sung Cho from the US. When the US facilitated foreign adoptions, including Indian, the children were promised a better life as American citizens. Adopted as children by US parents, an estimated 35,000 inter-country adoptees have grown up as Americans, like Jennifer, but still lack US citizenship.

In 2000, Congress determined that inter-country adoptees should automatically be granted US citizenship and the Childhood Citizenship Act (CCA) was passed. When the law went into effect, adoptees who were aged eighteen or older were denied the same automatic right. Jennifer unfortunately fell in this category then.

We call upon Congress to uphold the promise to adoptees by fixing the legal loophole and passing the Adoptee Citizenship Act of 2018, thereby allowing citizenship for all adoptees, regardless of when they were born. Fingers crossed, if the Bill is passed and this Act is implemented, then Jennifer will be able to return home to the US soon.

Karyn Schiller
Immigration Attorney
There is no such thing as a hardship visa. It doesn't exist. There is a humanitarian parole but it is harder to get than a waiver for a tourist visa. That was the best route for Jennifer. Also there might be a possibility of reopening Jennifer's case vis-à-vis the Sixth Circuit Rule, that the court may still have jurisdiction as the alien's departure from the US was not voluntary. The reason she was deported was because her citizenship was never processed completely as citizens, whether US or naturalized, can never be deported.

In Jennifer's case, the reason for her deportation was her second conviction. The judge found two drug misdemeanours (maximum possible punishment is less than a year unlike felony where the punishment exceeds over a year) and drug trafficking even though there was no intent to sell. If India had not been quick to take her, there would have been a Motion to Reconsider, but to file it she is needed in the US. Hence, humanitarian parole is needed to get her in as she is barred from the US for twenty years.

James Marsh
Senior Counsel
Jennifer can return to the US to vacate her drug convictions under Padilla, a significant court case in the US, since Jennifer was not informed of the deportation consequences of her guilty pleas. We also need to vacate her deportation order as her case is a major human rights violation case.

Justice Gyan Sudha Misra
Former Judge, Supreme Court of India
It was a harrowing story and I took an interest in this case and proceeded on the footing that if you are adopted by US parents and marry an American citizen, then it makes you a bona fide US citizen and you cannot be treated as an Indian and deported for felony.

However, it is still an arguable matter.

I see it more of a human and legal problem but must be treated with sensitivity and humaneness. If there is so much sympathy for terrorists, then why not for an unfortunate victim of circumstances?

If we go by the Supreme Court order whereby CARA has to ensure the adoptee be accorded the citizenship of the adopted country, then it is my appeal, that by drawing a parallel and analogy, the children who were sent out for adoption before this clause and the miniscule number who have not been accorded citizenship of their adopted country, like Jennifer, then by implication of this clause, they should also have similar rights. Like the pension hike laws applicable to all pensioners, this is a 'recurring law' and should be applicable to all, and not leave a few in the lurch.

Maneka Gandhi
Former Minister of Women and Child Development

The provisions in the present adoption laws are cumbersome and if the child is not adopted in the domestic front within 69 days then the child can be made available for inter-country adoption. However, the new law will cover offences against children who are illegally trafficked or sold, abducted, used for militant purposes and other child-related crimes. The idea behind these humane adoptive laws is to provide the child with a family environment which will be conducive to his or her growth. CARA should be accorded statutory status to function more effectively.

Jennifer's Appeal

I think about how I could never meet my mother because she died and she could not be reunited with me before I was deported to India. I hope that never happens with me and my children. I grew up not knowing my mother and the real cause for my adoption. That is the one life-long regret I will have.

I do not want my children to go through what I did. I do not want them to grow up not knowing their mother. I do not want them to feel unwanted and unloved as I did as a child.

I ask for you to understand, that while I have made mistakes, I have had ten years to reflect and better myself. Eight long years without seeing or hugging my children. I understand that I cannot come to the US on a permanent basis, but I just want the opportunity to see my children and develop a relationship with them.

Since I have been in India, I have become a stronger woman. Circumstances have forced me to do things I should not have, like hustling for a while, but then I had to keep body and soul together. Despite my financial hardships, I have not resorted to full-time drug peddling or other such dangerous stuff.

It was difficult, but some months ago I decided consciously not to hustle or sell drugs. And I have stuck to my decision since then. I have not even taken drugs in the last few months. Nor will I ever make those mistakes again.

I stayed in a shelter for distressed women when I came here and taught children who lived in the shelter and enjoyed it because they reminded me of my own children.

I have worked in BPOs but kept being thrown out and not given promotions because of lack of documentation. Even now getting a job has been difficult as the moment my employers Google me, they read my story, and want nothing to do with me.

My past seems to interfere with my present and no one seems to want to give me a second chance to secure and better my future. I think everyone deserves a second chance. Then why am I not getting it?

I am in touch with my children sometimes over the phone or on Skype, but it is hard to maintain a relationship with them over the phone. Currently, my daughter needs my presence around her as she is going through a difficult adolescence. The teachers feel that she needs the presence of her mother.

My mother-in-law, Judy Cobbs, has been taking care of my children in my absence. Since my husband, Justin Haynes, is also serving federal term, Judy has become a full-time parent to both my son and daughter. For this she has had to sacrifice her career, give up her job. However, she is getting on in age and of late, her health too has deteriorated.

With her failing health, it is difficult for her to manage the kids on her own. Her son, my husband, has still many years to serve in prison. At least, another twenty years or more to go. He will only be allowed out in the event of a death in the family, and that too on parole for a week at the most. If that happens, I shudder to think what will happen to my children, Kassana and Kadafi.

They will be put in foster care, will be separated and will go through the same shit I did in foster care. I don't want them to go to foster care. I don't want them to suffer there as I did. It is a vicious circle. Life is one big vicious circle, where the unfortunate are inundated with never-ending misfortunes!

Judy did send Kassana to live with me in India for a year. In 2017. That was probably the best year of my life in a long time. Initially, she loved it as much as I enjoyed the routine of motherhood, staying home, cooking for her and overseeing her studies. I was less of a mother and more of a friend. Kassana, an American, tried her best to adapt to the Indian environment. She took tuitions to learn the Hindi language. We put her in an IB school which was paid for by

Judy. But at 13, it was very difficult for her to adjust. Especially in Thane, located in the outskirts of Mumbai, where we live, the local children made fun of her in school. She missed her country, her home and her friends.

After a year of trying, she left for the US on 28 February 2018. Much as we both tried, India could never be her home. I am very sad…there's an emptiness without her. I feel homeless and without a family all over again.

Judy has said she would support me when I am home. She was so desperate to have me back, that she even pondered selling off her assets in the US and move on and settle in Canada with the children so that I would be able to join them. But, why should she leave her family and friends and country for no fault of her own?

I understand that I made mistakes I am not proud of. I am not proud of myself, and what I did with my earlier life. It was a hard and difficult time in my life and I was not strong enough to walk away from my husband's influence nor was I able to influence him away from such a life. Besides, my childhood had messed me up mentally and physically.

Having gone through so much and having lived in two countries, the country of my birth and the country of my adoption, I have seen enough to distinguish between the bad and good of both. I can now impart the best from both worlds to my children and help them grow up less dysfunctional.

I am stronger now. I have learnt my lesson. I will not repeat my mistakes.

I do not want my children to suffer because of what I did.

I hope I am reunited with my children soon. I hope I am able to return to a world I am familiar with. I hope I am able to be with my friends and family. I hope I am allowed to live like a free citizen with no restrictions.

I hope to live like a human being.

Mumbai, 2018

Epilogue

In July 2016, I had the pleasure of meeting Judy Cobbs when she visited India for the first time with Kadafi and Kassana. Jennifer was over the moon as she saw the reticent Kadafi, her little boy, for the first time since her deportation. It was a family reunion and Judy wanted Kassana to remain with Jennifer in India. It was a joint decision as she was impossible to handle and her teachers felt that as a teenager it would do her a world of good if she spent time with her biological mother. Besides, Judy could concentrate on Kadafi, whose grades were dropping.

Judy kept sending money for Kassana's education and upkeep. Jennifer moved into a bigger place and managed to buy a fridge and other household gadgets from the savings from the money Judy sent her. She even bought Kassana a bike, and Kassana zipped around Thane. Kassana enjoyed going to her school about 20 minutes from home, and her best friend in the international school was a Chinese girl. However she had difficulty in coping with her studies, especially the local languages, Hindi and Marathi.

For a year and a half, it was a happy time for Jenny. She, Austin and Kassana lived like one happy family, with their highs and lows and daily squabbles. Austin continued with his job. Kassana went to school and tuitions. And Jenny cooked and kept house for them. After school, Jenny helped Kassana with her schoolwork and on weekends they'd go out for movies and dinner. Many a time, Kassana, then thirteen going on twenty, and towering over the diminutive Jenny, would come over and we would explore the different eateries around the area.

One day Kassana called to say she wanted to meet me as she was leaving. 'Why?' I asked shocked. 'Well she needs to get back,'

Jenny explained. 'She needs to complete her education there. She's finding it difficult to cope up here.'

'But she could have tried. Give her time,' I asked, fearing Jenny would be devastated.

'Nope. She needs to be back,' Jenny said with finality.

Fearing a mother–daughter fallout, I asked Kassana whether she was okay with the idea, because Kassana always loved Mumbai as she felt wanted and loved here by Austin and Jenny, unlike in the US, where she felt Judy focused more on Kadafi than on her. Her rebellious ways was her protest against her neglect. She just shrugged. 'I'm okay.'

On 28 February 2018, Kassana flew back to the US.

I gave Jenny time to gather herself after Kassana's departure.

A fortnight later we met at the local diner by the sea, and spent a few languid hours over a lunch of pasta salad and chicken burgers and chocolate tart (which we both shared) with cups of Americano.

Jenny looked good. Slim. Calm and content. I had not seen her so relaxed in a long time. I told her so. She thanked me, blushing. Over lunch I asked her what was uppermost on my mind, 'Are you okay?'

'Course I am.'

'Don't you miss Kassana?'

'I did initially, but now I don't. I've gotten over that,' she said matter of fact. I nodded.

This was a complete different Jenny from the one I met almost four years ago, who craved for her children all the time.

'You see Naaeeta, when you met me four years ago, all I wanted was to get back home. All I missed were my children. I left them as babies and I was concerned about them. I know they missed me bad.

'But after meeting Kadafi and Kassana, I realized they have grown. I am their mother and they love me for that, but they have learnt to do without me. They grew up without me around. So they don't miss me that much.'

'I was happy to have Kassana with me but I realized she will have a much better education there and a much more comfortable life. Her future is there and I am not insecure about her feelings for me to stop that. I know she will always love me and come and spend holidays with me. I know Judy is getting on in years and cannot handle both of them together, so Kassana will stay with Chris, Justin's ex-girlfriend. She looked after the children while I was away serving correction term earlier when they were younger. She is two hours away from Judy and the children will meet over weekends and still have their space. It will be a lot easier on Judy. I know Chris will do well with Kassana.'

Pausing she added, 'Few years back, I was worried that should anything happen to Judy, my children would be separated and sent to different foster homes. I did not want them to go to foster homes. Man...that's real shit. I wouldn't be able to handle that. That would break my heart. When I was in foster care, I have seen siblings get split up from each other and I never wanted that. When I had Kadafi, I made up my mind that I would have another kid so that he would not be alone.'

'But today I know if anything bad were to happen, both are old enough to survive the bullshit. Kadafi will be 16 in a year's time, old enough to drive, and Kassana in two years' time. And man she is big and tough. Try messing with her,' Jenny laughs. 'Most important is that they know who their parents are.'

'And honestly Naaeeta, I don't give a f*ck whether I go back to the States or not. I don't want it that bad anymore. I'm happy here.' A revelation, which caught me by surprise.

Looking at my surprise she said, 'I know, I know. You must be shocked. But I'm 36 now. I've spent 10 years in this country. I love Mumbai. Legally, I can enter the States when I will be 45 but by then all my friends will have moved way ahead of me. I don't want to start life at 45. Or even at 40.

'Earlier I was worried for my children. Now I'm not.'

After a pause Jenny said, 'See, if I ever go back to the States, I would have to start all over again. When I was selling drugs in the States [note, she has started to refer to it as "the States" rather than "back home"], I had things like my own apartment, beautiful furniture and everything...but it was all drug money and it was taken away from me.'

'I came to this country with nothing and yeah it took a long time to get things like my fridge and my TV and my washing machine... but it is mine and not from drug money but my li'l earnings. If I go back, all my friends won't be the same coz they are 10 steps ahead of me.'

'I don't have anything to go back to. No place of my own. I'm 36 and I don't want to be 45 and starting all over again.'

'Don't get me wrong,' Jenny continues after a pause. 'I would love to have citizenship of the US, but not to live there but just to visit my kids and see them get married and see my grandkids in future. But I don't want to live there anymore...I'm comfortable living in India.'

※

On International Women's Day 2018, US Senators Roy Blunt (Montana) and Mazie Hirono (Hawaii) along with US representatives Adam Smith (Washington) and Chris Smith (New Jersey) introduced the bipartisan Adoptee Citizenship Act (ACA) of 2018. This legislation once passed will close a loophole in the Child Citizenship Act (CCA) of 2000, which has prevented internationally adopted children, who are now adults, like Jennifer, from receiving US citizenship despite being raised by American parents. By plugging the loophole in the CCA of 2000 by this current law, ACA of 2018, thousands of adoptees like Jennifer will have the security, stability and opportunity their adoptive parents intended for them when they welcomed them into their families.

Today, Jennifer may not bother much about going back to the

US, but she is lending her support to the ACA 2018, because she does not want others like her to suffer as she did.

It is a matter of a few years or more...who knows...but it will give Jennifer the freedom to travel and meet her family. And to live a life of dignity.

Postscript

Although Jennifer deserves a life of dignity after all the hardships she has had to suffer, it is easier said than done.

Whenever she goes for a job interview, the employers somehow manage to find out about her past—all it takes is a click on Google—and her chances of getting past ends right there. Yet, one has to survive. One has to sustain oneself. So peddling drugs is the only thing Jenny can go back to time and again.

On 16 July 2018, I got a call from Julietta that both Jennifer and her son, Austin, have been arrested for possession of drugs. They found it in Jenny's rented quarters, though Jenny insists she was not hustling. Austin was taken to Thane Central Jail while Jenny was whisked away to Byculla Women's Jail in Mumbai. Byculla is famous for housing some notorious women criminals including the dreaded Indrani Mukherjee, who is being held there on charges of killing her daughter, Sheena Bora.

Around August 2018, Pradeep and I visited her at Byculla. Jenny broke down saying, 'I'm sorry Naaeeta. I let you down.' She gathered herself and added, 'Get me out and I'll tell you the inside of an Indian jail. Not allowed to talk now. It's the pits is all I can say.'

On our way back, I asked Pradeep to apply for bail for her. He dismissed it saying, 'Much as I sympathize and empathize with Jenny, I want her to get rid of this hustling habit. Maybe a dose of Indian jails will help her rid of this. Besides, in three months' time, they will have prepared the charge sheet and in a couple of months' time she will be let out.'

Six months later on 21 January 2019 she was out on bail. She called me saying she had no clothes. I bought her some outfits and spent a whole afternoon at the mall with her. She was savouring every moment of freedom. We had a leisurely lunch at Chillies where she insisted on a couple of beers and her favourite spare ribs among other things.

Over lunch we chatted about her six months in Mumbai's Byculla jail. She was in Barrack No.1 measuring 25' x 15' sharing space with 52 other women. A typical day started with breakfast at 6 a.m., lunch at 9 a.m., tea at 11.30 a.m. and dinner at 1 p.m. At 2 p.m. the cells were locked till the next day! The food was just about okay with the usual fare of dal, rice, bhaji and chappati, with foreign nationals getting one ladi (about eight pieces) of pao (bread) for the whole day. At times 'you got maggots in your food', she says in a matter-of-fact way. She befriended a couple of Nigerian women, and an Arab girl held for possession of narcotics like her.

Amongst her close friends were two Gujrati girls, Tina and Twinkle. They stole cell phones from passengers in the local trains and gave them to their boyfriends who sold them and gave them a cut. Tina did the Nalasopara trains while Twinkle handled the Churchgate locals. Between them they had stolen over 90 mobile phones till they got caught. In jail, they discovered they shared the same boyfriend who was cheating on them simultaneously. They got together, spilled the beans on him and finally the police caught him. He is currently serving term in Thane central for rape! He is yet to be convicted. Tina and Twinkle have served their term and are out.

Her fellow inmates included Bollywood producer Prerna Arora of KriArj Entertainment (producer for the Bollywood flicks *Rustom* and *Toilet: Ek Prem Katha*) serving term for a sixteen crore rupees fraud. 'Prerna is a damn good dancer and taught me to dance.' As also Anita Apaya, who is serving for killing her husband, a hockey player. 'Apparently they argued over her boyfriend post sex and she was so bugged she stabbed him 14 times. So she says,' Jenny explains. 'But she's a damn good friend of Indrani. Indrani Mukherjee. She colours her [Indrani's] hair for her each month with the henna they buy from the prison shop.'

Indrani Mukherjee née Bora hit the headlines in August 2015 when the Mumbai police arrested her for the murder of her daughter, Sheena Bora. Known as the better half of ex-Star TV head honcho, India's Rupert Murdoch, Peter Mukherjee, Indrani had a colourful past before she married Peter. Coming from a poor family in Guwahati, Indrani left behind a couple of husbands and a brood of children to marry the wealthy aging magnate. Amongst them were her two children from her first husband, Sheena and Mikhail Bora, whom she introduced as her siblings.

Due to her alliance with Peter she moved up the social ladder in India and Europe, while her children Sheena and Mikhail were surviving a hand-to-mouth existence. Fearing exposure, Indrani was forced to help her children financially, but when the demands from Sheena grew, Indrani with the help of her driver and second husband killed her daughter sometime in April 2012. Sheena's body was discovered three years later.

For weeks together, the Sheena Bora murder case made headlines. Apart from Indrani, her driver and second husband were arrested along with 'the much respected' Peter Mukherjee, for abetment to murder.

According to Jennifer, 'Without make-up and her grey hair she looks like in her sixties. After Anita dyes her hair she looks in her fifties. Though she has a private cell measuring 4' x 8', there are two guards checking on her as well as CCTV cameras as she tried committing suicide a couple of times. She is on heavy anti-depressants. There's no special food for her, just regular fare but she eats inside her cell. She's a poor eater. But she writes a lot.'

Jennifer was made to share the room with Indrani for about 10 days. 'Initially, she was curt. Then she opened up a bit talking about her travels worldwide and her interaction with Bollywood stars. Shahrukh Khan is cool for her but she finds Salman has an attitude. Her first husband was a good man but a drunkard, while the second was quite chilled out. She says that she prefers the UK to India and that she's going to be out of jail in a couple of years and settle in Bristol. And she says it was Peter who helped kill her daughter along with her!'

'Of course, Anita told me a different story. But, Indrani maintains Peter and she together killed the girl. When I asked her whether it haunted her killing her own child, she said initially it did, but now it doesn't anymore. She used to take a lot of Codine [cough syrup] and shared some with me when I was her roomie.'

As of now, Jennifer continues to live in a paying guest accommodation in Thane. Austin is out now though his bail was rejected thrice. Austin continues to visit Jenny. They are still a couple though they aren't married. They say they don't hustle. I don't know whether to believe them or not. Judy continues to help Jenny off and on and pay for the children. Kadafi stays with Judy and Kassana is with her friend Chris. Justin's still serving the last leg of his prison term. And Clarice D'Souza, well into her nineties, continues to live a peaceful life in her sea-facing Mumbai apartment after having disrupted the lives of thousands of innocent children. Roelie Post, Arun Dohle, Pradeep Havnur and others like them are still trying to fight against child trafficking!

I can only hope and pray life is peaceful for Jennifer henceforth.

To me Jennifer Haynes is not only a representation of the millions of illegal inter-country adoptees, but also a representation of human suffering. And yet despite it all, she is the epitome of the Darwinian philosophy of the survival of the fittest.

And survived, she most certainly has. What she deserves now is to live with dignity.

Acknowledgments

First of-all, I would like to thank Pradeep Havnur for having faith in me to write Jennifer's story and helping me in every part of this journey.

For Sushovan Banerjee, for prodding me to start writing the book from the beginning to the middle and till the very end! Without your encouragement, this book would perhaps never have seen the light of day.

Arun Dohle for always being there to fill in the gaps.

Judy Cobbs, Justin Haynes and Jennifer's family and friends in the US.

Austin Rozario and her friends in India.

The Rupa team.

My son, Ishaan, always a pillar of quiet support.

My staff at home. And supportive friends.

My husband, Om Puri, who is no more but who has always encouraged me to push the boundaries. I miss you a lot.

My late mother, Sati Chowdhury. I miss you, Ma.

Above all, Jennifer Pinky Francis Anne Hancox Edgell Haynes. Thank you, my friend. Hope you find your happy space.